The Huge Book of Amazing Facts

by
Jake Jacobs

* * * * *

Published by Jake Jacobs

1.

William Hooper was one of the signers of the United States Declaration of Independence.

2.

He was born on June 28, 1742, in Boston, Massachusetts.

3.

Hooper's parents were immigrants from Scotland who settled in America.

4.

He attended Harvard College and graduated in 1760 with a Bachelor of Arts degree.

5.

Hooper studied law and was admitted to the bar in 1764, practicing in North Carolina.

6.

He became involved in local politics and was elected to the North Carolina Provincial Congress in 1774.

7.

Hooper was known for his eloquence and persuasive speaking abilities.

8.

He was a strong advocate for American independence and played a key role in the drafting of the Mecklenburg Resolves, a precursor to the Declaration of Independence.

9.

Hooper was elected to the Continental Congress in 1774 and served until 1777.

10.

As a delegate to the Continental Congress, Hooper was a vocal critic of British policies and played a crucial role in shaping the early foundations of the United States.

11.

Hooper was a member of the committee responsible for drafting the Articles of Confederation.

12.

He was a strong supporter of a centralized government and the establishment of a strong executive branch.

13.

Hooper was known for his conservative political views and was often at odds with more radical members of Congress.

14.

During his time in Congress, Hooper worked on various committees, including the Committee on Indian Affairs.

15.

He was one of the three North Carolina signers of the Declaration of Independence, along with Joseph Hewes and John Penn.

16.

Hooper's signature on the Declaration of Independence is widely regarded as one of the most legible and distinctive.

17.

Hooper's commitment to the cause of independence came at great personal sacrifice. He left behind his family and property in North Carolina to join the Continental Congress.

18.

In 1776, Hooper's home in North Carolina was destroyed by British troops as an act of retaliation for his role in the revolution.

19.

Hooper's wife, Ann Clark Hooper, remained in North Carolina during his time in Congress and managed their estate.

20.

Hooper's tenure in Congress was marked by financial difficulties. He struggled to support his family and was often in debt.

21.

Despite his financial struggles, Hooper was known for his integrity and refused bribes and offers of financial assistance that could compromise his position.

22.

After leaving Congress in 1777, Hooper returned to North Carolina and resumed his law practice.

23.

He served as a judge on the North Carolina Superior Court from 1782 until his death.

24.

Hooper was an early advocate for the abolition of slavery and publicly spoke out against the institution.

25.

He believed that slavery was incompatible with the principles of liberty and equality.

26.

Hooper's anti-slavery stance was met with resistance in the South, where the institution of slavery was deeply entrenched.

27.

Hooper's health began to decline in the 1780s, and he suffered from various ailments, including kidney disease.

28.

He died on October 14, 1790, at the age of 48, in Hillsborough, North Carolina.

29.

Hooper was buried in the Hooper family cemetery, which is now part of the Historic Hillsborough Cemetery.

30.

In 1894, a statue of William Hooper was erected in his honor in downtown Wilmington, North Carolina.

31.

Hooper's legacy as a Founding Father and signer of the Declaration of Independence is celebrated in his home state of North Carolina.

32.

He is remembered as a principled and dedicated patriot who played a crucial role in the fight for American independence.

33.

Hooper's writings and speeches continue to be studied by historians and scholars interested in the Revolutionary era.

34.

Several buildings and institutions in North Carolina bear Hooper's name, including the William Hooper Building at the University of North Carolina at Chapel Hill.

35.

Hooper's life and contributions to American history have been commemorated on postage stamps and in various works of art.

36.

He is often mentioned alongside other prominent Founding Fathers, such as George Washington, Thomas Jefferson, and John Adams.

37.

Hooper's descendants have played notable roles in American history, including his great-grandson, William Henry Belk, who founded the Belk department store chain.

38.

Hooper's commitment to public service and his dedication to the principles of liberty continue to inspire generations of Americans.

39.

He is remembered for his unwavering belief in the rights and freedoms of individuals and his tireless efforts to secure those rights for all Americans.

40.

Hooper's contributions to the formation of the United States laid the groundwork for the democratic principles that still guide the nation today.

41.

His legacy serves as a reminder of the sacrifices made by the Founding Fathers and the importance of civic engagement in shaping the future of a nation.

42.

Hooper's portrait has been featured in numerous historical exhibitions and is often displayed alongside other Founding Fathers in museums and educational institutions.

43.

His speeches and writings continue to be studied and quoted by scholars and enthusiasts interested in the history of the American Revolution.

44.

Hooper's dedication to public service and his willingness to put the interests of the nation above his own personal gain serve as a model for future leaders.

45.

He believed in the power of individual liberty and the importance of a limited government that protects the rights and freedoms of its citizens.

46.

Hooper's contributions to the American Revolution were recognized by his contemporaries and continue to be celebrated today.

47.

His commitment to the cause of independence inspired others to join the fight for liberty and shaped the course of American history.

48.

Hooper's influence extended beyond his political career. He was known for his intellectual pursuits and contributed to the fields of law and philosophy.

49.

His writings on government and natural rights were influential in shaping the political philosophy of the time and continue to be studied by scholars.

50.

Hooper's legacy as a patriot, statesman, and defender of individual rights lives on, reminding us of the principles on which the United States was founded and inspiring future generations to uphold those principles.

51.

The Allis shad, also known as the Alosa alosa, is a species of fish belonging to the herring family.

52.

It is found in the Eastern Atlantic Ocean, primarily in the rivers of Western Europe.

53.

Allis shad are anadromous fish, meaning they migrate from the ocean to freshwater rivers to spawn.

54.

They have a streamlined body shape with a silver-green color and a dark spot behind their gill cover.

55.

Allis shad can reach lengths of up to 60 centimeters (24 inches) and weigh up to 2 kilograms (4.4 pounds).

56.

They are known for their strong migratory instincts and can travel long distances to reach their spawning grounds.

57.

Allis shad are known for their leaping ability and can jump several feet out of the water.

58.

They are primarily a nocturnal species, feeding mainly on small fish and invertebrates.

59.

Allis shad spawn in freshwater rivers during the spring and early summer months.

60.

Females release thousands of eggs, which are fertilized externally by males.

61.

After spawning, the adults return to the sea, and the young fish, known as fry, remain in the rivers until they are ready to migrate.

62.

Allis shad populations have declined significantly over the past century due to habitat loss, pollution, and overfishing.

63.

They are now considered a protected species in many countries and are listed as endangered or critically endangered in some regions.

64.

Efforts are being made to restore Allis shad populations through habitat restoration and conservation initiatives.

65.

Allis shad are an important species ecologically as they provide a food source for other predators, including birds and larger fish.

66.

They have a complex life cycle, spending different stages of their life in both freshwater and marine environments.

67.

The Allis shad is named after the English physician and naturalist Thomas Allis, who first described the species in the 19th century.

68.

The species has a long history of cultural significance, being celebrated in traditional festivals and folklore in some regions.

69.

Allis shad are highly valued by anglers for their sport fishing qualities.

70.

They are known for their powerful and acrobatic fights when hooked.

71.

The fish has a delicate flavor and is considered a culinary delicacy in some countries.

72.

Allis shad are known to make distinctive clicking sounds during their spawning migrations, which are thought to be communication signals.

73.

The species has a high level of genetic diversity, indicating its adaptation to different river systems and habitats.

74.

Allis shad have been successfully introduced to some rivers outside their natural range as part of conservation efforts.

75.

They have been reintroduced to rivers in England, France, and Portugal, among other countries.

76.

Allis shad have a lifespan of around 8 to 10 years.

77.

The fish have a well-developed sense of smell, which helps them navigate to their spawning grounds.

78.

They have a relatively high tolerance for varying water salinity levels, allowing them to adapt to different environments.

79.

Allis shad are highly sensitive to changes in water temperature, which can affect their reproductive success.

80.

The fish exhibit schooling behavior, gathering in large groups during migration and spawning.

81.

Allis shad are known to undertake extensive migrations, with some individuals traveling hundreds of kilometers to reach their spawning grounds.

82.

They are capable of jumping over weirs and small waterfalls to continue their upstream journey.

83.

Allis shad populations are monitored closely by fisheries biologists to assess their conservation status and inform management practices.

84.

The fish play a role in nutrient cycling in freshwater ecosystems, as their carcasses provide food for other organisms.

85.

Allis shad have been studied extensively by researchers interested in their biology, behavior, and conservation.

86.

They are considered an indicator species, meaning their presence or absence can indicate the overall health of an aquatic ecosystem.

87.

Allis shad are listed as a priority species under the European Union's Habitats Directive, highlighting their conservation importance.

88.

The species is part of ongoing research projects aimed at understanding their migratory behavior and the factors influencing their population decline.

89.

Allis shad are known to exhibit site fidelity, returning to the same spawning grounds each year.

90.

The fish have a keen sense of orientation and can navigate using various cues, including the Earth's magnetic field.

91.

Allis shad are occasionally caught as bycatch in commercial fishing operations targeting other species.

92.

Efforts are being made to reduce bycatch mortality through the use of selective fishing gear and practices.

93.

The fish are susceptible to pollution and habitat degradation, making them particularly vulnerable to human-induced environmental changes.

94.

Allis shad are often studied in conjunction with other diadromous fish species, such as salmon and eels, to understand broader patterns of migration and ecosystem dynamics.

95.

The species has been successfully bred in captivity for research and conservation purposes.

96.

Allis shad eggs and larvae require specific conditions to hatch and develop, making captive breeding programs challenging.

97.

The fish have a unique scale pattern, which can be used to identify individuals and study population dynamics.

98.

Allis shad exhibit sexual dimorphism, with males generally being larger and more brightly colored than females.

99.

The species has been the subject of traditional fishing practices and cultural celebrations in some regions, reflecting its historical importance to local communities.

100.

Allis shad have captured the fascination of naturalists, anglers, and conservationists alike, symbolizing the resilience and beauty of migratory fish species in the face of environmental challenges.

101.

Leffingwell Camp Site is located in the Arctic region of Alaska, specifically on the Arctic Ocean coast of Alaska's North Slope.

102.

It was established in 1909 by geologist and explorer Ernest de Koven Leffingwell during the U.S. Naval Petroleum Reserve No. 4 survey.

103.

The campsite served as a base for Leffingwell's geological research and mapping of the region.

104.

Leffingwell Camp Site is considered a significant historical site for its role in the early exploration and understanding of the Arctic.

105.

The campsite is situated near the modern-day village of Kaktovik, which is known for its Inupiaq community and rich cultural heritage.

106.

Leffingwell's work at the campsite contributed to the knowledge of the region's geology, permafrost, and ice dynamics.

107.

Leffingwell's detailed observations and recordings at the campsite helped advance scientific understanding of the Arctic environment.

108.

The campsite consists of the remains of Leffingwell's expedition structures, including buildings and equipment.

109.

It is an important archaeological site, providing valuable insights into early Arctic exploration and scientific research practices.

110.

Leffingwell's campsite is often visited by researchers, historians, and those interested in Arctic exploration.

111.

The campsite offers a glimpse into the challenges and hardships faced by early explorers in the harsh Arctic conditions.

112.

Leffingwell's observations of coastal erosion at the campsite helped contribute to the understanding of climate change impacts in the Arctic.

113.

The campsite is part of the Arctic National Wildlife Refuge, which is known for its diverse wildlife and pristine natural beauty.

114.

Leffingwell Camp Site is recognized as a National Historic Landmark due to its historical and scientific significance.

115.

The campsite provides a unique opportunity to study the cultural and scientific history of the Arctic and its impact on local communities.

116.

Leffingwell's pioneering work at the campsite laid the foundation for subsequent Arctic research and exploration efforts.

117.

The campsite offers a scenic view of the Arctic Ocean and the surrounding tundra landscape.

118.

It serves as a reminder of the determination and perseverance of early explorers in their quest for knowledge and understanding of the Arctic.

119.

Leffingwell's research at the campsite included the study of permafrost, which is a crucial aspect of the Arctic ecosystem.

120.

The campsite's location in a remote and pristine environment provides a sense of solitude and connection with nature.

121.

Leffingwell's publications based on his work at the campsite contributed to scientific literature on Arctic geology and glaciology.

122.

The campsite serves as a historical marker of the changing Arctic environment and the impact of human activities on the region.

123.

It offers opportunities for outdoor activities such as hiking, birdwatching, and photography.

124.

Leffingwell Camp Site is a testament to the spirit of exploration and scientific inquiry that has shaped our understanding of the Arctic.

125.

The campsite's archaeological remains include artifacts and structures that provide insights into the daily life of early Arctic explorers.

126.

Leffingwell's campsite is a popular destination for educational field trips, allowing students to learn about Arctic history and scientific research.

127.

The campsite is part of ongoing efforts to preserve and protect historical and cultural sites in the Arctic region.

128.

Leffingwell's work at the campsite contributed to the recognition of the Arctic as a unique and important ecosystem.

129.

The campsite is an important site for interdisciplinary research, bringing together scientists from various fields to study the Arctic environment.

130.

Leffingwell's campsite serves as a symbol of resilience and adaptation, highlighting the ability of humans to thrive in extreme environments.

131.

The campsite offers opportunities for camping and experiencing the rugged beauty of the Arctic landscape.

132.

Leffingwell's observations of glaciers near the campsite provided valuable data on their movement and dynamics.

133.

The campsite is a reminder of the rich cultural history of the indigenous people who have inhabited the Arctic for thousands of years.

134.

Leffingwell's campsite is one of the few remaining structures from the early 20th-century Arctic expeditions.

135.

The campsite's location on the coast allows for the study of coastal processes, such as erosion and sedimentation.

136.

Leffingwell's work at the campsite helped establish the scientific foundation for subsequent Arctic expeditions and research programs.

137.

The campsite serves as a point of interest for those interested in the history of Arctic exploration and scientific discoveries.

138.

Leffingwell's campsite provides an opportunity to reflect on the changes that have occurred in the Arctic over the past century.

139.

The campsite's proximity to the Arctic Ocean offers the chance to observe marine wildlife and ice formations.

140.

Leffingwell's campsite is a place of inspiration for artists, writers, and photographers seeking to capture the beauty of the Arctic landscape.

141.

The campsite's preservation and interpretation efforts contribute to public awareness and appreciation of the Arctic's natural and cultural heritage.

142.

Leffingwell's campsite is a focal point for scientific collaborations and international research initiatives focused on the Arctic.

143.

The campsite provides a platform for studying the effects of climate change on Arctic ecosystems and biodiversity.

144.

Leffingwell's campsite is a reminder of the importance of sustainable practices in the Arctic and the need to protect its fragile environment.

145.

The campsite offers opportunities for guided tours and interpretive programs, allowing visitors to learn about the campsite's history and significance.

146.

Leffingwell's campsite serves as a research hub for studying the Arctic's geological history and its implications for understanding Earth's past climate.

147.

The campsite's location within the Arctic Circle makes it an ideal site for studying polar phenomena such as the midnight sun and auroras.

148.

Leffingwell's campsite is a place of solitude and reflection, allowing visitors to connect with the vastness and beauty of the Arctic landscape.

149.

The campsite's remote location provides an escape from the busy world, offering a serene and untouched environment.

150.

Leffingwell's campsite is a testament to the human fascination with the Arctic and the ongoing quest to unravel its mysteries.

151.

The Nenana was a river steamboat that operated on the Yukon River in Alaska during the early 20th century.

152.

It was built in 1933 by the White Pass and Yukon Route railroad company to transport passengers and cargo along the river.

153.

The Nenana was named after the Nenana River, a tributary of the Tanana River in Alaska.

154.

It was one of the largest and most powerful sternwheelers on the Yukon River, measuring 237 feet in length.

155.

The steamboat had a capacity to carry up to 300 passengers and 300 tons of cargo.

156.

The Nenana played a crucial role in supplying remote communities and mining operations along the Yukon River.

157.

It transported essential goods such as food, fuel, and building materials to remote areas of Alaska.

158.

The steamboat was powered by a steam engine, with two large paddlewheels on its sides propelling it through the water.

159.

The Nenana's steam engine produced 2,100 horsepower, allowing it to navigate the strong currents and shallow waters of the Yukon River.

160.

It had a maximum speed of around 16 miles per hour.

161.

The Nenana operated during the summer months when the river was free of ice, typically from May to September.

162.

The steamboat made regular trips between the towns of Nenana and Dawson City, covering a distance of over 500 miles.

163.

It provided a vital lifeline for isolated communities, delivering mail, supplies, and news from the outside world.

164.

The Nenana's large cargo holds were capable of carrying a wide range of goods, including machinery, livestock, and even automobiles.

165.

Passengers on the Nenana enjoyed comfortable accommodations, with sleeping berths, dining facilities, and even a small library onboard.

166.

The steamboat's crew consisted of skilled navigators, engineers, and deckhands who ensured the safe and efficient operation of the vessel.

167.

The Nenana was equipped with wireless telegraphy, allowing communication with other steamboats and land-based stations.

168.

Despite its large size and power, the Nenana was maneuverable enough to navigate through narrow channels and bends in the river.

169.

The steamboat's paddlewheels were sometimes used to break through thin ice on the river during early spring and late fall.

170.

The Nenana became a symbol of transportation and connection in the remote regions of Alaska.

171.

It played a significant role in supporting the growth of mining operations along the Yukon River, transporting miners, equipment, and supplies.

172.

The steamboat's presence brought economic development to communities along its route, facilitating trade and commerce.

173.

The Nenana was a familiar sight on the Yukon River, and its arrival at a town or settlement was met with anticipation and excitement.

174.

The steamboat's journey was not without challenges, as it had to navigate treacherous sections of the river, including rapids and shallow areas.

175.

The Nenana's hull was reinforced with steel plates to withstand potential collisions with floating ice and debris.

176.

The steamboat was a popular subject for photographers and artists, capturing its grandeur and significance in Alaska's history.

177.

The Nenana played a role in transporting supplies and equipment during the construction of the Alaska Highway in the 1940s.

178.

The steamboat's operations declined with the advent of roads and improved transportation infrastructure in the region.

179.

In 1955, the Nenana was retired from active service and was eventually preserved as a historic artifact.

180.

The Nenana is now on display at the Pioneer Park in Fairbanks, Alaska, where visitors can explore its decks and learn about its history.

181.

The steamboat serves as a reminder of the pioneering spirit and resilience of those who relied on river transportation in Alaska's early days.

182.

The Nenana's preservation allows future generations to appreciate the challenges and achievements of early river travel in the wilderness of Alaska.

183.

The steamboat's iconic paddlewheels and elegant design make it a popular subject for model ship enthusiasts.

184.

The Nenana's historical significance extends beyond its role as a river steamboat—it represents a bygone era of transportation and exploration.

185.

The steamboat's legacy lives on through photographs, documents, and personal stories that provide a glimpse into the past.

186.

The Nenana's operational period coincided with the decline of other sternwheelers on the Yukon River, making it one of the last of its kind.

187.

The steamboat's cargo capacity made it an essential lifeline for remote communities that depended on regular deliveries of supplies.

188.

The Nenana's steam-powered machinery was a marvel of engineering at the time, showcasing the ingenuity and craftsmanship of its builders.

189.

The steamboat's steam whistle could be heard echoing along the river, announcing its arrival and departure.

190.

The Nenana's journey was not without dangers, including the risk of striking submerged rocks and snags hidden beneath the river's surface.

191.

The steamboat's paddlewheels churned up large amounts of water, creating a distinctive sound and leaving a trail of foam in its wake.

192.

The Nenana's crew included skilled river pilots who had an intimate knowledge of the river's currents, sandbars, and hazards.

193.

The steamboat's spacious decks provided a gathering place for passengers, offering a unique vantage point to enjoy the passing scenery.

194.

The Nenana's operations contributed to the growth of communities along the Yukon River, fostering trade and social connections.

195.

The steamboat's arrival often marked a festive occasion, with locals gathering on the riverbanks to welcome its passengers and witness its grandeur.

196.

The Nenana's boilers required a constant supply of fuel, typically wood or coal, to generate the steam necessary for propulsion.

197.

The steamboat's stately appearance and graceful movement on the water evoked a sense of elegance and adventure.

198.

The Nenana's journeys brought people from diverse backgrounds together, fostering a sense of community and shared experiences.

199.

The steamboat's regular schedule provided a reliable means of transportation for those who lived along the river, enabling them to access essential services and resources.

200.

The Nenana's legacy as a symbol of Alaska's river transportation era lives on, reminding us of the pioneering spirit and determination of those who navigated the challenging waters of the Yukon River.

201.

William Hooper was born on June 28, 1742, in Boston, Massachusetts.

202.

He was one of the signers of the United States Declaration of Independence.

203.

Hooper attended Harvard College, where he studied law and graduated with honors.

204.

After completing his education, he moved to Wilmington, North Carolina, where he established a successful law practice.

205.

Hooper became involved in local politics and was elected to represent North Carolina in the Continental Congress.

206.

He was known for his eloquent speeches and strong support for American independence.

207.

Hooper played a key role in drafting and debating the Declaration of Independence, advocating for the rights and freedoms of the American people.

208.

As a member of the Congress, Hooper also served on various committees, including the Committee on Foreign Affairs and the Committee on Indian Affairs.

209.

Hooper was a strong advocate for religious freedom and believed in the separation of church and state.

210.

He was a staunch supporter of the American Revolution and actively worked to rally support for the cause.

211.

During the Revolutionary War, Hooper's property was confiscated by the British, and his family was forced to flee for their safety.

212.

Hooper was known for his integrity and honesty, and he was highly respected by his colleagues in Congress.

213.

He was a skilled writer and contributed to several influential publications, including the Cape Fear Mercury, where he published articles promoting American independence.

214.

Hooper was instrumental in shaping the legal and political systems of North Carolina, playing a significant role in drafting the state's first constitution.

215.

He served as North Carolina's Attorney General from 1777 to 1781, working to establish a fair and just legal system.

216.

Hooper was a strong advocate for education and believed in the importance of an educated citizenry for the success of the new nation.

217.

He was one of the founders of the University of North Carolina at Chapel Hill and served on the university's board of trustees.

218.

Hooper was known for his eloquence and persuasive speaking abilities, which made him a compelling figure in the fight for independence.

219.

He was a proponent of economic independence and advocated for American industries to thrive and compete on the global stage.

220.

Hooper's dedication to the cause of independence came at great personal sacrifice, as he put his own safety and well-being at risk for the sake of his country.

221.

He was deeply committed to the principles of liberty and justice, advocating for equal rights for all citizens, regardless of their background.

222.

Hooper was a strong supporter of the abolition of slavery and believed that all individuals should be treated with dignity and respect.

223.

After the war, Hooper returned to his legal practice and continued to serve the people of North Carolina.

224.

He was appointed as a federal judge by President George Washington in 1790, a position he held until his death.

225.

Hooper was known for his sharp intellect and keen legal mind, earning him a reputation as one of North Carolina's most distinguished lawyers.

226.

He was a devoted family man and had a close and loving relationship with his wife and children.

227.

Hooper's commitment to public service extended beyond his political career, as he was actively involved in charitable and community organizations.

228.

He was a strong advocate for the rights of Native Americans and worked to improve their living conditions and protect their land rights.

229.

Hooper's legal expertise and knowledge of constitutional law made him a valuable resource for his colleagues in Congress.

230.

He was a member of the committee that drafted the Articles of Confederation, the first constitution of the United States.

231.

Hooper's contributions to the formation of the new nation extended beyond his role as a signer of the Declaration of Independence.

232.

He played a key role in the establishment of the federal court system and the development of the American legal system.

233.

Hooper was a man of integrity and honor, and his colleagues described him as a principled and trustworthy leader.

234.

He believed in the power of the law to protect individual rights and ensure a just society.

235.

Hooper's commitment to public service was driven by his belief in the importance of civic duty and the responsibility of citizens to participate in the governance of their country.

236.

He was a skilled diplomat and represented the United States in negotiations with foreign nations, working to secure favorable trade agreements and promote American interests.

237.

Hooper's dedication to the principles of liberty and freedom inspired future generations of Americans to fight for their rights and uphold the values of the nation.

238.

He was a prolific writer and his correspondence with his colleagues and friends provides valuable insights into the political and social climate of the time.

239.

Hooper's legacy as a founding father of the United States is celebrated and remembered for his contributions to the establishment of a free and independent nation.

240.

His name is immortalized in history as one of the signatories of the Declaration of Independence, a document that symbolizes the aspirations and ideals of the American people.

241.

Hooper's life and career are a testament to the power of individual action and the impact that one person can have on the course of history.

242.

He is remembered as a patriot, a statesman, and a champion of liberty, whose dedication and sacrifices laid the foundation for the nation we know today.

243.

Hooper's commitment to justice and equality serves as an inspiration to future generations to fight for the rights and freedoms of all people.

244.

His legacy lives on in the principles and values that continue to guide the United States, reminding us of the importance of standing up for what is right and just.

245.

Hooper's contributions to the founding of the nation are honored and celebrated in North Carolina, where he is remembered as one of the state's most influential and respected leaders.

246.

His life story serves as a reminder that ordinary individuals can make extraordinary contributions to the betterment of society.

247.

Hooper's legal expertise and dedication to the rule of law helped shape the legal system of the United States, ensuring that justice is accessible to all.

248.

He was known for his unwavering commitment to his principles and his refusal to compromise on matters of integrity and ethics.

249.

Hooper's leadership and eloquence made him a trusted and influential voice in the fight for independence, inspiring others to join the cause.

250.

His contributions to the founding of the United States, both as a signer of the Declaration of Independence and as a champion of liberty and justice, are a testament to his enduring legacy.

251.

The Alpine ibex (Capra ibex) is a species of wild mountain goat native to the European Alps.

252.

It is one of the largest ibex species, with males weighing between 65 to 100 kg (143 to 220 lbs) and females weighing between 40 to 60 kg (88 to 132 lbs).

253.

The Alpine ibex is known for its impressive curved horns, which can grow up to 1 meter (3.3 feet) long in males.

254.

Both males and females have horns, but the male horns are larger and more impressive.

255.

The horns of the Alpine ibex are used for defense, territorial disputes, and attracting mates during the breeding season.

256.

The ibex's horns grow throughout its life and are composed of keratin, the same material found in human fingernails.

257.

The Alpine ibex has a sturdy and muscular build, well-suited for climbing steep rocky terrain.

258.

They are excellent climbers and can scale almost vertical slopes with ease.

259.

The hooves of the ibex have a rubbery sole that provides them with excellent grip on rocky surfaces.

260.

The ibex has a unique adaptation called dewclaws, which are extra digits located on the back of their legs. These help provide extra stability while climbing.

261.

Their fur is typically brown in color, blending well with the rocky surroundings of their habitat.

262.

During the winter months, their fur becomes thicker and provides insulation against the cold weather.

263.

The Alpine ibex is herbivorous and primarily feeds on grasses, herbs, shrubs, and lichens.

264.

They have a specialized digestive system that allows them to extract nutrients from the low-quality vegetation found in their habitat.

265.

The ibex is well adapted to the harsh alpine environment, with its dense fur, strong body, and ability to withstand extreme temperatures.

266.

In the summer, the ibex migrates to higher elevations where the vegetation is more abundant, and descends to lower elevations during the winter.

267.

The mating season for Alpine ibex occurs in late fall, and males engage in dramatic displays of dominance to attract females.

268.

During the mating season, males clash their horns together in aggressive displays, creating loud echoes that can be heard across the mountain slopes.

269.

The dominant males, known as "masters," have the highest reproductive success and mate with multiple females.

270.

The gestation period for Alpine ibex is around 5 to 6 months, and females give birth to a single kid in the spring.

271.

Newborn ibexes are able to walk shortly after birth and are well-developed.

272.

The kids stay close to their mothers and form strong bonds with them.

273.

Alpine ibex have a lifespan of around 15 to 20 years in the wild.

274.

They are social animals and live in herds, which are usually segregated by sex, with males and females forming separate groups.

275.

The herd structure helps protect against predators and provides greater vigilance against potential threats.

276.

The ibex has few natural predators in its mountainous habitat, but golden eagles and lynxes are known to prey on young and weak individuals.

277.

The population of Alpine ibex declined significantly in the 19th and early 20th centuries due to hunting and habitat loss.

278.

Conservation efforts and reintroduction programs have helped restore their populations in several regions of the Alps.

279.

The Alpine ibex is now listed as a species of "Least Concern" on the IUCN Red List of Threatened Species.

280.

They are considered an important symbol of the mountainous regions and are often depicted in local folklore and art.

281.

The ibex is a popular subject for wildlife photographers and nature enthusiasts due to its striking appearance and impressive climbing abilities.

282.

It has been the subject of scientific research on topics such as adaptation to high-altitude environments and social behavior.

283.

Alpine ibex are known for their agility and have been observed leaping up to 6 feet vertically and 8 feet horizontally.

284.

They have excellent eyesight and can detect predators from a distance, allowing them to take evasive action.

285.

The ibex has a keen sense of smell, which helps them locate food and detect the presence of predators.

286.

They communicate with each other through a variety of vocalizations, including grunts, snorts, and alarm calls.

287.

During the winter months, when food is scarce, the ibex relies on stored body fat for energy.

288.

They have a specialized digestive system that allows them to extract maximum nutrition from their food.

289.

The ibex has an efficient water conservation mechanism, and it can obtain most of its water requirements from the moisture in the plants it consumes.

290.

The Alpine ibex has adapted to living in high-altitude environments, where oxygen levels are lower, by developing a larger lung capacity.

291.

They have a thick layer of fat under their skin, known as blubber, which provides insulation and helps regulate body temperature.

292.

The ibex sheds its horns annually, and new ones start growing immediately afterward.

293.

The discarded horns of the ibex are highly valued and are used in traditional crafts and decorative items.

294.

The ibex is an important ecological component of the alpine ecosystem, as it helps control vegetation growth through grazing.

295.

Their presence helps maintain the balance between plant communities and prevents the domination of certain plant species.

296.

The ibex is a highly adaptable species and has been successfully introduced into other mountainous regions outside of its native range.

297.

They have been observed engaging in playful behavior, such as chasing each other and engaging in mock battles.

298.

The ibex has a hierarchical social structure, with dominant individuals enjoying better access to resources and mating opportunities.

299.

They have a unique grooming behavior where they rub their horns and bodies against trees and rocks to mark their territory and leave scent cues for other ibexes.

300.

The Alpine ibex serves as a flagship species for the conservation of alpine ecosystems and highlights the importance of preserving these fragile mountain habitats.

301.

The Amazon river dolphin, also known as the pink river dolphin or boto, is a species of freshwater dolphin found in the rivers of the Amazon and Orinoco basins in South America.

302.

It is one of the largest river dolphin species, with males growing up to 8 feet in length and weighing around 300 pounds.

303.

The Amazon river dolphin has a distinctive pink coloration, which is more pronounced in males. Juveniles are usually gray and gradually develop the pink color as they mature.

304.

The pink color is due to the dolphin's blood vessels being close to the surface of the skin, which gives it a flushed appearance.

305.

The skin of the Amazon river dolphin is extremely delicate and sensitive, and it is believed that the pink color helps with thermoregulation.

306.

These dolphins have a flexible neck that allows them to move their heads in various directions, aiding in maneuvering through the complex riverine habitats.

307.

The Amazon river dolphin has a long, slender body, a prominent forehead, and a curved dorsal fin.

308.

They have sharp teeth designed for catching fish, their primary source of food.

309.

Amazon river dolphins are highly intelligent and have a complex social structure. They live in groups called pods, which can range in size from a few individuals to over 100.

310.

Within a pod, dolphins engage in cooperative hunting, communication, and social interactions.

311.

They are known for their vocalizations, which include clicks, whistles, and body slaps, used for communication and echolocation.

312.

The Amazon river dolphin has a flexible neck vertebrae that enables it to rotate its head up to 180 degrees, providing excellent maneuverability in the dense vegetation of the Amazon basin.

313.

They are primarily nocturnal, being most active during the early morning and late afternoon hours.

314.

The diet of the Amazon river dolphin consists mainly of fish, including catfish, piranhas, and various species found in the river systems.

315.

They have a unique feeding technique known as "herding," where they use their bodies to create pressure waves, corralling fish into shallow areas for easier capture.

316.

Unlike marine dolphins, the Amazon river dolphin has a flexible jaw joint that allows it to move each half of its lower jaw independently, facilitating efficient feeding on slippery prey.

317.

The reproductive cycle of Amazon river dolphins is closely tied to the annual flooding of the rivers. They give birth during the dry season when water levels are lower and food resources are more concentrated.

318.

Female dolphins have a gestation period of around 11 to 12 months, and they usually give birth to a single calf, which is nursed for several months.

319.

The calves have a grayish coloration and gradually develop the pink coloration as they mature.

320.

The Amazon river dolphin is known for its playful behavior, often seen jumping and splashing in the water.

321.

They are excellent swimmers and can reach speeds of up to 15 miles per hour.

322.

The Amazon river dolphin has adapted to its freshwater environment with a specialized kidney system that allows it to filter out excess water and maintain proper salt balance.

323.

They have a long lifespan, with individuals living up to 30 years in the wild.

324.

The pink coloration of the Amazon river dolphin can vary depending on factors such as age, sex, and individual health.

325.

The species is sexually dimorphic, with males being larger and having more pronounced pink coloration than females.

326.

Amazon river dolphins have been culturally significant to indigenous communities in the Amazon basin, with various myths and legends surrounding them.

327.

They play an important ecological role as top predators, helping to maintain the balance of fish populations in the river systems.

328.

The Amazon river dolphin is classified as a vulnerable species by the International Union for Conservation of Nature (IUCN) due to habitat loss, pollution, and accidental entanglement in fishing gear.

329.

Conservation efforts are underway to protect their habitat and ensure their long-term survival.

330.

They are protected by law in several countries within their range, including Brazil, Peru, and Colombia.

331.

The unique coloration and graceful movements of the Amazon river dolphin make it a popular subject for ecotourism, attracting visitors from around the world.

332.

They are skilled navigators and can navigate through complex river systems using their echolocation abilities.

333.

The Amazon river dolphin has a large melon, a fatty structure on its forehead, which aids in echolocation and communication.

334.

They have a highly developed sense of touch and can detect subtle vibrations in the water, helping them locate prey and navigate in their environment.

335.

Amazon river dolphins have been observed engaging in cooperative behaviors, such as herding fish together for a shared meal.

336.

They have a remarkable ability to adapt to changing water levels during the annual flood cycles, allowing them to access new feeding areas and exploit different resources.

337.

The Amazon river dolphin has a unique breeding behavior called "sexual barking," where males produce loud vocalizations to attract females during the mating season.

338.

They are known to be curious and have been observed investigating objects and interactions with humans in some cases.

339.

The species has specialized adaptations for living in murky river waters, including well-developed eyes and a highly sensitive auditory system.

340.

Amazon river dolphins have been observed using tools, such as sticks, to dislodge fish from underwater crevices.

341.

They have a strong bond with their pod members and often engage in social grooming, where they rub against each other to strengthen social bonds and remove parasites.

342.

The species is known to be highly resilient, capable of surviving in different river habitats, including flooded forests, open channels, and oxbow lakes.

343.

The Amazon river dolphin has been a subject of scientific research to understand their social structure, communication, and ecological role in the ecosystem.

344.

They are able to navigate through complex river systems by using landmarks and memorizing specific routes.

345.

The Amazon river dolphin is often depicted in traditional art and folklore of indigenous cultures in the Amazon basin.

346.

They are known to display a range of behaviors, including breaching, tail-slapping, and spy-hopping (poking their heads out of the water) to observe their surroundings.

347.

Amazon river dolphins have a layered social structure, with large pods consisting of smaller groups that exhibit cooperative behaviors.

348.

The species has been studied for its unique vocalizations, which are distinct from other dolphin species and may serve as a means of individual recognition and communication.

349.

The Amazon river dolphin is an indicator species, meaning its presence and health can indicate the overall ecological well-being of the river systems they inhabit.

350.

Conservation efforts are aimed at protecting the Amazon river dolphin's habitat, reducing pollution, and raising awareness about the importance of preserving their unique and fragile ecosystem.

351.

Herbert Hoover was the 31st President of the United States, serving from 1929 to 1933.

352.

He was born on August 10, 1874, in West Branch, Iowa.

353.

Hoover graduated from Stanford University in 1895 with a degree in geology.

354.

Before entering politics, Hoover worked as a mining engineer and made a fortune in the mining industry.

355.

Hoover gained worldwide recognition for his humanitarian efforts during and after World War I, coordinating relief efforts in Europe and helping to feed millions of people.

356.

He served as the Secretary of Commerce under Presidents Warren G. Harding and Calvin Coolidge.

357.

Hoover's presidency was overshadowed by the Great Depression, which began shortly after he took office in 1929.

358.

He implemented various policies to combat the economic downturn, but his efforts were largely unsuccessful in alleviating the crisis.

359.

Hoover's approach to the Great Depression emphasized individualism and voluntary cooperation rather than direct government intervention.

360.

He signed the Smoot-Hawley Tariff Act in 1930, which raised tariffs on imported goods and contributed to the worsening of global trade.

361.

Hoover established the Reconstruction Finance Corporation to provide emergency loans to struggling banks, railroads, and other businesses.

362.

Despite his efforts, unemployment continued to rise, and the economy spiraled further into depression during his presidency.

363.

Hoover's response to the Bonus Army, a group of World War I veterans demanding early payment of their bonuses, was widely criticized. He ordered their eviction from their makeshift camps in Washington, D.C., which led to a violent clash.

364.

Hoover lost the 1932 presidential election to Franklin D. Roosevelt in a landslide.

365.

After leaving office, Hoover remained active in public life, writing books, giving speeches, and providing advice to subsequent presidents.

366.

He played a significant role in the organization and administration of relief efforts during World War II.

367.

Hoover was a strong advocate for volunteerism and emphasized the importance of individual initiative and self-reliance.

368.

He established the Hoover Institution at Stanford University in 1919, which focuses on public policy research and analysis.

369.

Hoover was the first President to have a telephone on his desk in the Oval Office.

370.

He was known for his love of fishing and spent much of his free time pursuing the sport.

371.

Hoover and his wife, Lou Henry Hoover, were avid conservationists and worked to preserve natural resources and national parks.

372.

He was the last President to have been born in the 19th century.

373.

Hoover spoke Mandarin Chinese fluently and worked as a mining engineer in China early in his career.

374.

During his presidency, Hoover implemented the Hoover Moratorium, a temporary suspension of war debt payments to alleviate economic strain.

375.

He had a deep interest in engineering and was involved in numerous engineering projects throughout his life.

376.

Hoover advocated for prison reform and believed in providing opportunities for rehabilitation and education for inmates.

377.

Hoover was the first President to have a formal White House Press Secretary.

378.

He was a skilled public speaker and often used radio addresses to communicate with the American people.

379.

Hoover was known for his meticulous attention to detail and his hands-on approach to governance.

380.

He was a staunch opponent of communism and worked to combat its spread both domestically and internationally.

381.

Hoover was an accomplished author and published several books on a wide range of topics, including mining, engineering, and history.

382.

He was an advocate for international peace and played a role in the establishment of the United Nations.

383.

Hoover served as the chairman of the Commission for the Organization of Executive Branch of Government, which led to significant government reorganization efforts.

384.

He was instrumental in the establishment of the Federal Bureau of Investigation (FBI) and supported its efforts to combat organized crime.

385.

Hoover was an early proponent of aviation and believed in the importance of developing a strong aviation industry.

386.

He was the first President to have a presidential aircraft, known as the "Sacred Cow."

387.

Hoover received numerous honors and awards throughout his life, including the Nobel Peace Prize in 1947 for his humanitarian work.

388.

He was known for his frugal lifestyle and refused to accept a presidential salary during his time in office.

389.

Hoover was an amateur geologist and made significant contributions to the field, including the discovery of new minerals.

390.

He was a strong advocate for civil rights and worked to improve conditions for African Americans, particularly in education and employment.

391.

Hoover was a progressive Republican and believed in the power of private enterprise and limited government intervention.

392.

He was an early supporter of women's suffrage and actively campaigned for the passage of the 19th Amendment.

393.

Hoover and his wife were the first Presidential couple to have a telephone line installed in their personal residence.

394.

He was known for his ability to speak multiple languages, including Mandarin Chinese, Latin, and French.

395.

Hoover's presidency coincided with the beginning of the Prohibition era, and he supported the enforcement of alcohol prohibition laws.

396.

He was an advocate for vocational education and believed in the importance of practical skills for the workforce.

397.

Hoover was the first President to have his inauguration broadcast on the radio.

398.

He served as the chairman of the Boys' Clubs of America, now known as the Boys & Girls Clubs of America.

399.

Hoover's childhood home in West Branch, Iowa, is now a national historic site and museum.

400.

He passed away on October 20, 1964, at the age of 90, in New York City.

401.

Stephen Hopkins was one of the signers of the Declaration of Independence, representing Rhode Island.

402.

He was born on March 7, 1707, in Providence, Rhode Island.

403.

Hopkins was the only person to have signed the Declaration of Independence for Rhode Island and later served as its governor.

404.

He had a diverse political career and held various positions, including town clerk, speaker of the Rhode Island House of Representatives, and chief justice of the Rhode Island Supreme Court.

405.

Hopkins was a self-taught scholar and had a deep interest in science, astronomy, and mathematics.

406.

He corresponded with notable scientists of his time, such as Benjamin Franklin and Thomas Jefferson, exchanging ideas and observations.

407.

Hopkins played a crucial role in the establishment of the University of Rhode Island and served as its first chancellor.

408.

He was a vocal opponent of British taxation policies and became an active participant in the revolutionary movement.

409.

Hopkins attended the Stamp Act Congress in 1765, where he was one of the signers of the Stamp Act Resolves, protesting against the taxation measures.

410.

During the American Revolution, Hopkins served in the Continental Congress and was a member of the committee responsible for drafting the Articles of Confederation.

411.

Hopkins was chosen as one of the signers of the Declaration of Independence due to his reputation for being a skilled orator and a fervent advocate for independence.

412.

He suffered from a condition called palsy, which caused his hands to shake. Despite this, he managed to affix his signature to the Declaration of Independence.

413.

Hopkins was the only signer of the Declaration of Independence who later served as governor of his state.

414.

He played a significant role in the ratification of the United States Constitution in Rhode Island.

415.

Hopkins was an advocate for religious freedom and was influential in securing religious liberty provisions in the Rhode Island State Constitution.

416.

He was a supporter of the abolitionist movement and took steps towards ending slavery in Rhode Island during his governorship.

417.

Hopkins was known for his wit and sense of humor, often using these qualities to defuse tension during debates and negotiations.

418.

He had a reputation for being a man of integrity and honesty, earning the respect of his peers.

419.

Hopkins was a close friend and political ally of Samuel Adams, another prominent figure in the American Revolution.

420.

He was part of the delegation that negotiated the Treaty of Paris in 1783, officially ending the Revolutionary War and securing American independence.

421.

Hopkins retired from politics in 1786 and spent his later years in private life, focusing on his personal interests and family.

422.

He had a large family, with nine children from his first marriage and seven children from his second marriage.

<h1 style="text-align:center">423.</h1>

Hopkins had a keen interest in maritime affairs and served as a commissioner of the Rhode Island Admiralty Court.

<h1 style="text-align:center">424.</h1>

He was known for his love of books and amassed an extensive personal library, which he generously shared with others.

<h1 style="text-align:center">425.</h1>

Hopkins was an early advocate for women's education and supported the establishment of schools for girls.

<h1 style="text-align:center">426.</h1>

He had a deep appreciation for Native American culture and advocated for fair treatment of indigenous peoples.

<h1 style="text-align:center">427.</h1>

Hopkins' home in Providence, Rhode Island, known as the Stephen Hopkins House, still stands today and is a National Historic Landmark.

<h1 style="text-align:center">428.</h1>

Hopkins' political career spanned over five decades, making him one of the longest-serving politicians of his time.

<h1 style="text-align:center">429.</h1>

He was a strong proponent of individual liberties and believed in limited government intervention.

<h1 style="text-align:center">430.</h1>

Hopkins' contribution to the founding of the United States earned him a place in history as one of the Founding Fathers.

<h1 style="text-align:center">431.</h1>

He passed away on July 13, 1785, at the age of 78, in Providence, Rhode Island.

432.

Hopkins' grave is located at the North Burial Ground in Providence, and his tombstone bears an inscription honoring his role in the American Revolution.

433.

He is remembered as a dedicated patriot who played a crucial role in shaping the early years of the United States.

434.

Hopkins' legacy lives on through his numerous writings and contributions to the development of Rhode Island and the nation.

435.

His life story and contributions continue to inspire scholars and historians, shedding light on the struggles and triumphs of the Revolutionary era.

436.

Hopkins' dedication to the principles of liberty and justice continues to resonate with Americans today.

437.

His commitment to public service and his unwavering support for the American cause set an example for future generations of leaders.

438.

Hopkins' influence extended beyond politics and law; his intellectual pursuits and scientific interests left a lasting impact on the fields of astronomy and mathematics.

439.

He was a staunch defender of the rights of individuals and believed in the power of the people to govern themselves.

440.

Hopkins' efforts to promote education and intellectual growth helped shape the intellectual landscape of Rhode Island and the nation.

441.

He was known for his kindness and compassion, often providing support and assistance to those in need.

442.

Hopkins' dedication to the principles of freedom and equality made him a champion for marginalized communities and a voice for social justice.

443.

He was admired for his wisdom and sound judgment, often sought out for advice and guidance by his colleagues.

444.

Hopkins' commitment to public service was unwavering, and he never hesitated to put the needs of the nation above his personal interests.

445.

He played a crucial role in shaping the early legislative framework of Rhode Island, working to establish a government that upheld the principles of democracy and individual rights.

446.

Hopkins' tireless efforts to secure American independence earned him the respect and admiration of his fellow patriots.

447.

He was a skilled negotiator and diplomat, known for his ability to find common ground and build consensus.

448.

Hopkins' contributions to the development of Rhode Island's legal system helped establish a foundation for the rule of law and the protection of individual rights.

449.

He was a strong advocate for free trade and worked to promote economic growth and prosperity in Rhode Island.

450.

Hopkins' unwavering commitment to the ideals of liberty, justice, and equality left an indelible mark on the history of Rhode Island and the nation as a whole.

451.

New Russia Site is an archaeological site located in Essex County, New York, United States.

452.

The site is of significant historical and cultural importance, representing the early European settlement in the region.

453.

It was established by Count Nikolay Rezanov, a prominent Russian diplomat, as part of a Russian colonization effort in North America.

454.

The settlement was founded in 1792 and served as a trading post and agricultural community.

455.

New Russia Site is situated along the Bouquet River and features a mix of archaeological remains and reconstructed structures.

456.

The site includes a reconstructed Russian Orthodox church, known as the "Church of the Holy Ascension," which stands as a testament to the Russian presence in the area.

457.

The settlement was strategically located to facilitate trade between the Russian Empire and the indigenous peoples of the region.

458.

The residents of New Russia engaged in fur trapping, agriculture, and trade with Native American tribes.

459.

The site showcases a unique blend of Russian, Native American, and European cultural influences.

460.

New Russia Site offers visitors a glimpse into the daily lives and activities of the early Russian settlers and the interactions between different cultures.

461.

The archaeological excavations at the site have unearthed various artifacts, including tools, pottery, and personal items, shedding light on the material culture of the settlers.

462.

The New Russia Site is listed on the National Register of Historic Places, recognizing its historical significance and preserving its heritage.

463.

The settlement's location in the Adirondack Mountains provides a scenic backdrop and offers opportunities for outdoor recreation and exploration.

464.

The New Russia Site serves as a cultural and educational center, hosting events, workshops, and demonstrations to educate visitors about the site's history and significance.

465.

The Russian Orthodox church at the site continues to hold religious services, providing a place of worship for local residents and visitors.

466.

New Russia Site serves as a reminder of the diverse cultural heritage and history of the region, fostering an appreciation for the contributions of different communities.

467.

The site has been the subject of ongoing research and archaeological investigations to uncover more details about the early Russian settlement.

468.

Visitors to New Russia Site can learn about the challenges and successes faced by the settlers, gaining insight into the complexities of frontier life.

469.

The site offers guided tours and interpretive exhibits that highlight the unique aspects of the Russian settlement and its significance in North American history.

470.

New Russia Site is surrounded by natural beauty, with opportunities for hiking, birdwatching, and other outdoor activities in the nearby Adirondack Park.

471.

The settlement played a role in the fur trade, with fur traders establishing relationships with Native American tribes to procure valuable pelts.

472.

New Russia Site represents an important chapter in the history of Russian exploration and colonization in North America.

473.

The settlers at New Russia faced challenges such as harsh weather conditions, limited resources, and the need to adapt to unfamiliar environments.

474.

The site provides a glimpse into the daily lives and customs of the Russian settlers, including their clothing, food, and social interactions.

475.

New Russia Site is part of a larger network of historic sites and attractions in the Adirondack region, offering visitors a rich cultural and historical experience.

476.

The New Russia Site serves as a gathering place for descendants of the early Russian settlers, who come together to celebrate their shared heritage.

477.

The settlement's location near the Bouquet River provided access to transportation and facilitated trade with neighboring communities.

478.

New Russia Site serves as a living history museum, with reenactors and interpreters portraying the daily activities of the early settlers.

479.

The site's architecture reflects the unique blend of Russian and American influences, creating a distinct visual identity.

480.

New Russia Site is a place of cultural exchange, where Native American tribes and Russian settlers shared knowledge, traditions, and goods.

481.

The Russian settlers at New Russia played a role in the development of local industries, including logging, farming, and fishing.

482.

The site's historical significance extends beyond the Russian settlement period, with evidence of Native American presence and earlier human activity in the area.

483.

New Russia Site provides opportunities for visitors to participate in hands-on activities, such as traditional crafts, cooking, and music.

484.

The settlement's proximity to the Adirondack Mountains offered the settlers access to natural resources and recreational opportunities.

485.

New Russia Site is an example of the global connections and influences that shaped the history of North America.

486.

The site's preservation and interpretation efforts are supported by local organizations, volunteers, and community members dedicated to preserving its heritage.

487.

New Russia Site attracts researchers and scholars interested in studying the Russian colonization efforts and their impact on local history and culture.

488.

The site's landscape features a mix of open fields, forests, and waterways, providing diverse habitats for wildlife and opportunities for nature enthusiasts.

489.

New Russia Site is a popular destination for photographers, artists, and filmmakers seeking to capture the beauty and historical significance of the area.

490.

The settlement's location in the heart of the Adirondacks offers visitors a chance to explore the region's natural wonders, including hiking trails, lakes, and scenic drives.

491.

New Russia Site represents an era of exploration and discovery, where individuals from different backgrounds ventured into unknown territories in search of new opportunities.

492.

The site's exhibits and educational programs explore the cultural exchange and interactions between the Russian settlers, Native American tribes, and later European immigrants.

493.

New Russia Site serves as a reminder of the resilience and adaptability of the early settlers, who faced numerous challenges in their quest to establish a thriving community.

494.

The site's natural surroundings provide a peaceful and serene atmosphere, allowing visitors to connect with nature and reflect on the historical significance of the area.

495.

New Russia Site offers opportunities for volunteer work and community engagement, allowing individuals to contribute to the preservation and promotion of its heritage.

496.

The settlement's economic activities included farming, hunting, trapping, and trade, contributing to the local economy and providing sustenance for the community.

497.

New Russia Site is a place of pilgrimage for individuals interested in exploring their ancestral roots and connecting with their Russian heritage.

498.

The site's archaeological discoveries continue to shed light on the daily lives of the settlers, offering insights into their social structures, religious practices, and cultural traditions.

499.

New Russia Site serves as a gathering place for cultural festivals, events, and celebrations, fostering a sense of community and appreciation for the region's diverse history.

500.

The ongoing preservation efforts at New Russia Site ensure that future generations can continue to learn about and be inspired by the stories and contributions of the early Russian settlers in the Adirondack region.

501.

Old Sitka, also known as the "Old Sitka Site," is an archaeological site located in Sitka, Alaska, United States.

502.

The site is of historical and cultural significance as it was the location of the first Russian settlement in Alaska.

503.

Old Sitka was established in 1799 as a trading post and administrative center by the Russian-American Company.

504.

The settlement was strategically located on the west coast of Baranof Island, providing access to valuable natural resources and trade routes.

505.

Old Sitka served as the capital of Russian America for several years before it was relocated to nearby Sitka.

506.

The settlement played a crucial role in the fur trade industry, with fur traders and indigenous peoples engaging in commerce and cultural exchange.

507.

The Russian Orthodox Church played a central role in the community, with the establishment of the St. Michael's Cathedral at Old Sitka.

508.

Old Sitka was home to a diverse population, including Russian fur traders, Native Alaskans, and Aleut and Tlingit peoples.

509.

The site features archaeological remains, including the foundations of buildings, fortifications, and artifacts, providing insights into the daily life of the settlers.

510.

Old Sitka was the site of significant historical events, including conflicts between the Russian settlers and the indigenous Tlingit people.

511.

The Battle of Sitka in 1804 marked a major turning point in the history of the region, resulting in the transfer of control from the Tlingit to the Russians.

512.

The settlement's location on the coast offered access to abundant seafood resources, including fish, shellfish, and sea mammals.

513.

Old Sitka was an important center for the Russian Orthodox Church, with religious ceremonies, baptisms, and weddings taking place at St. Michael's Cathedral.

514.

The settlement's architecture showcased a blend of Russian and Native Alaskan influences, with log buildings and traditional indigenous designs.

515.

Old Sitka's natural surroundings are characterized by dense forests, mountains, and scenic views, creating a picturesque backdrop for the historic site.

516.

The site's preservation efforts aim to protect the remaining structures and artifacts, ensuring the continued appreciation of its historical significance.

517.

Visitors to Old Sitka can explore the site's interpretive exhibits and guided tours, learning about the history and cultural significance of the settlement.

518.

The area surrounding Old Sitka is rich in wildlife, offering opportunities for birdwatching, hiking, and nature photography.

519.

Old Sitka serves as a place of cultural and historical education, hosting workshops, lectures, and traditional craft demonstrations.

520.

The settlement's strategic location along the Pacific coast played a role in facilitating trade between Russia, Asia, and North America.

521.

Old Sitka's history is intertwined with the natural environment, as the settlers relied on the region's resources for sustenance and trade.

522.

The settlement's economy was supported by activities such as fur trapping, hunting, fishing, and agriculture.

523.

Old Sitka's cultural landscape reflects the interactions between Russian settlers and the indigenous peoples, including the adoption of local customs and traditions.

524.

The relocation of the capital from Old Sitka to the current city of Sitka marked a transition in the region's governance and administration.

525.

The archaeological investigations at Old Sitka continue to uncover new insights into the early Russian settlement and its impact on the local population.

526.

The site's historical significance is recognized by its inclusion on the National Register of Historic Places.

527.

Old Sitka serves as a place of reflection and remembrance, commemorating the individuals who shaped the early history of the region.

528.

The settlement's decline was attributed to various factors, including conflicts with the indigenous population, changing economic dynamics, and shifts in the fur trade industry.

529.

Old Sitka's ruins stand as a testament to the resilience and perseverance of the early settlers in adapting to a challenging environment.

530.

The site's natural beauty and historical significance make it a popular destination for tourists interested in exploring Alaska's rich cultural heritage.

531.

Old Sitka's role as a trading post contributed to the exchange of goods, ideas, and technologies between different cultures and regions.

532.

The establishment of Old Sitka marked Russia's territorial expansion into North America and the beginning of its colonization efforts in the region.

533.

The settlement's location on Baranof Island provided access to abundant timber resources, which were used for construction and trade.

534.

Old Sitka's archaeological excavations have uncovered artifacts such as pottery, tools, and personal items, shedding light on the material culture of the early settlers.

535.

The Tlingit people, who had a long-standing presence in the area, played a significant role in the interactions and conflicts with the Russian settlers at Old Sitka.

536.

The transfer of control from Russia to the United States in 1867 as part of the Alaska Purchase marked a significant shift in the region's political landscape.

537.

Old Sitka's history is intertwined with the broader context of colonialism, trade networks, and geopolitical interests of the 19th century.

538.

The site's natural resources, including forests, rivers, and marine ecosystems, supported the subsistence and livelihoods of the early settlers.

539.

Old Sitka's landscape offers opportunities for outdoor activities such as camping, boating, and wildlife observation.

540.

The site's proximity to the Tongass National Forest provides visitors with access to pristine wilderness areas and hiking trails.

541.

Old Sitka's historical significance extends beyond the Russian colonial period, with evidence of human habitation dating back thousands of years.

542.

The Russian-American Company, which established Old Sitka,
played a central role in the economic and political affairs of the
region during the 19th century.

543.

Old Sitka's cultural heritage is celebrated through events and
festivals that showcase traditional music, dance, and crafts of the
indigenous peoples.

544.

The settlement's architecture incorporated elements of both Russian
and indigenous building techniques, reflecting the blending of
cultures in the region.

545.

Old Sitka's coastal location made it susceptible to natural disasters
such as storms and tsunamis, which had an impact on the
development and survival of the settlement.

546.

The site's significance as the first Russian settlement in Alaska is
recognized by its designation as a National Historic Landmark.

547.

Old Sitka's history is preserved and interpreted through partnerships
between local communities, government agencies, and cultural
organizations.

548.

The site's historical narratives include stories of exploration, trade,
colonization, and the struggles faced by both the Russian settlers and
the indigenous populations.

549.

Old Sitka's natural environment provides a habitat for a variety of wildlife, including eagles, bears, marine mammals, and salmon.

550.

The ongoing archaeological research and interpretation at Old Sitka continue to enhance our understanding of the region's past and its significance in the broader context of Alaskan history.

551.

The Amazonian Manatee, also known as the South American Manatee, is a large aquatic mammal found in the rivers and wetlands of the Amazon basin.

552.

They are herbivorous animals, primarily feeding on aquatic plants, grasses, and fruits that grow near the water's edge.

553.

Amazonian Manatees are the smallest of the three species of manatees, with adults typically reaching lengths of 8 to 10 feet and weighing around 800 to 1,200 pounds.

554.

These manatees have a round, barrel-shaped body with paddle-like flippers and a flattened tail that helps them navigate through the water.

555.

They have a grayish-brown or grayish-black coloration, which helps them blend in with their surroundings.

556.

Amazonian Manatees are highly adapted to their aquatic lifestyle, with nostrils located on the top of their snout, allowing them to breathe while the rest of their body remains submerged.

557.

They have a specialized sense of touch, with sensitive bristles on their face and upper lip that help them locate and grasp vegetation.

558.

Amazonian Manatees are known for their slow movements and gentle nature, often referred to as the "gentle giants" of the Amazon.

559.

They are social animals and are often found in small groups or solitary individuals.

560.

Amazonian Manatees have a unique reproductive strategy known as "delayed implantation." After mating, the fertilized egg remains dormant in the female's uterus for several months before implanting and starting development.

561.

The gestation period for Amazonian Manatees is around 12 to 14 months, one of the longest among mammals.

562.

Newborn Amazonian Manatees, called calves, weigh around 40 to 60 pounds and are about 3 feet long.

563.

Calves stay close to their mothers for up to two years, learning essential survival skills and feeding behaviors.

564.

These manatees are primarily found in freshwater environments, including rivers, lakes, and flooded forests.

565.

They are well adapted to the low-oxygen conditions of the Amazon basin, with the ability to hold their breath for several minutes.

566.

Amazonian Manatees have a slow metabolic rate, allowing them to conserve energy in their relatively low-nutrient habitat.

567.

These manatees have a specialized digestive system that allows them to efficiently extract nutrients from their plant-based diet.

568.

They play a vital role in maintaining the health of their ecosystem by acting as ecosystem engineers, helping to control vegetation growth and promoting biodiversity.

569.

Amazonian Manatees are considered a flagship species for conservation efforts in the Amazon basin, as their presence indicates the overall health of the aquatic environment.

570.

Threats to the Amazonian Manatee include habitat loss due to deforestation, dam construction, and pollution from agricultural runoff and mining activities.

571.

They are also at risk from accidental entanglement in fishing nets and collisions with boats.

572.

The Amazonian Manatee is listed as a vulnerable species by the International Union for Conservation of Nature (IUCN) due to population decline and habitat degradation.

573.

Conservation efforts are underway to protect their habitat and reduce human-induced threats through initiatives such as protected areas, community-based conservation programs, and public awareness campaigns.

574.

The Amazonian Manatee is protected by law in many countries within its range, including Brazil, Colombia, and Peru.

575.

Research on Amazonian Manatees is ongoing to better understand their behavior, habitat requirements, and population dynamics.

576.

They have a unique vocal repertoire, using a variety of vocalizations to communicate with each other, including chirps, whistles, and grunts.

577.

Amazonian Manatees have a lifespan of around 30 to 50 years in the wild.

578.

They have a relatively low reproductive rate, with females typically giving birth to one calf every two to five years.

579.

These manatees have a thick layer of blubber that provides insulation and buoyancy in the water.

580.

Their skin is rough and wrinkled, with algae often growing on their backs, providing camouflage in their natural habitat.

581.

Amazonian Manatees have a high tolerance for temperature fluctuations and can adapt to both warm and cool water environments.

582.

They are excellent swimmers and can reach speeds of up to 15 miles per hour in short bursts.

583.

Amazonian Manatees are known to migrate between different river systems in search of food and suitable breeding grounds.

584.

They have few natural predators in the wild, with the main threats coming from human activities.

585.

These manatees have large, sensitive lips that they use to grasp and manipulate vegetation.

586.

Amazonian Manatees have a unique dental structure, with continuously growing molars that are adapted for grinding tough vegetation.

587.

They have well-developed senses of hearing and touch, which help them navigate their environment and locate food.

588.

These manatees have been historically hunted for their meat, oil, and skin, but hunting is now strictly regulated or prohibited in most countries.

589.

The Amazonian Manatee has cultural significance for indigenous communities living along the rivers, with traditional stories and beliefs associated with these gentle creatures.

590.

They are often referred to by local names such as "peixe-boi" in Brazil and "vacas marinas" in Colombia.

591.

Amazonian Manatees are known to bask in the sun near the water's surface to regulate their body temperature.

592.

They have a unique reproductive anatomy, with females having two mammary glands located near their armpits to nurse their young.

593.

These manatees have a slow metabolic rate and can survive for long periods without feeding.

594.

Amazonian Manatees have been studied for their potential as bioindicators of water quality and ecosystem health.

595.

They have a complex social structure, with individuals forming long-term bonds and engaging in cooperative behaviors.

596.

These manatees have been observed using tools, such as using their flippers to dig for food or to protect themselves from the sharp edges of underwater obstacles.

597.

Amazonian Manatees have a unique breeding season, typically occurring during the dry season when water levels are lower.

598.

They are highly sensitive to changes in their environment, including water pollution and noise pollution from human activities.

599.

These manatees have a slow reproductive rate, making them particularly vulnerable to population decline.

600.

Efforts are underway to raise awareness about the importance of protecting Amazonian Manatees and their habitats, with the goal of ensuring their long-term survival in the wild.

601.

The American badger (Taxidea taxus) is a medium-sized mammal native to North America.

602.

They are part of the Mustelidae family, which also includes weasels, otters, and ferrets.

603.

American badgers have a stocky build with short legs and a broad body.

604.

They have a distinct coloration, with a grizzled gray coat featuring a white stripe that extends from their head to their tail.

605.

Their head is flat and wedge-shaped, with a pointed snout and small ears.

606.

American badgers are highly adapted diggers and have strong, muscular forelimbs and long, sharp claws that allow them to excavate burrows and dig for prey.

607.

They are solitary animals and have large territories, with males typically having larger ranges than females.

608.

American badgers are primarily nocturnal but may also be active during the day, especially during the cooler months.

609.

They are opportunistic predators and have a diet that mainly consists of small mammals, such as ground squirrels, mice, voles, and rabbits.

610.

Badgers are known for their remarkable digging skills and can quickly excavate extensive burrow systems called setts.

611.

Their burrows can be quite complex and may include multiple entrances, tunnels, and chambers for different purposes, including nesting, caching food, and providing shelter.

612.

American badgers are known for their strong jaws and teeth, which they use to crush the skulls of their prey.

613.

They have keen senses of smell and hearing, which help them locate prey underground.

614.

American badgers are not strong runners but can reach speeds of up to 20 miles per hour in short bursts.

615.

They are also excellent swimmers and can cross bodies of water when necessary.

616.

American badgers are known for their aggressive defense of their territory. When threatened, they can emit growls, hisses, and snarls.

617.

Despite their aggressive reputation, American badgers generally avoid confrontation and will retreat to their burrows when confronted by larger predators.

618.

They have been observed displaying "hopping" behavior, where they stand on their hind legs and bounce up and down, possibly to intimidate predators or communicate with other badgers.

619.

American badgers have a low reproductive rate, with females typically giving birth to one to five young, known as kits, in a litter.

620.

The kits are born blind and helpless, and their eyes open after about 4 weeks.

621.

Young badgers stay with their mother until they are around 4 to 5 months old and then venture out on their own.

622.

American badgers have a lifespan of around 4 to 10 years in the wild.

623.

They have been known to use abandoned burrows of other animals, such as prairie dogs or ground squirrels, as temporary shelters.

624.

Badgers play an important ecological role by controlling rodent populations, which can have significant impacts on ecosystems.

625.

They are considered a keystone species in some habitats due to their influence on the abundance and distribution of other species.

626.

American badgers are found throughout much of North America, from Canada to Mexico, in a variety of habitats, including grasslands, prairies, deserts, and open woodlands.

627.

They are highly adaptable and can survive in different climates and soil conditions.

628.

Badgers have a unique behavior called "caching," where they store excess food in their burrows for later consumption.

629.

They are known for their ability to excavate burrows in hard and compacted soils, sometimes even breaking through frozen ground.

630.

American badgers have a strong scent gland located near the base of their tail, which they use for marking their territory and communicating with other badgers.

631.

They have a specialized flap of skin called a "dewlap" on their throat, which they can inflate and display during territorial disputes or courtship displays.

632.

American badgers are not considered endangered, but their populations have faced some declines due to habitat loss and fragmentation.

633.

They are protected by laws and regulations in many states and provinces throughout their range.

634.

In Native American folklore, the badger is often associated with bravery, strength, and healing powers.

635.

The American badger is the state animal of Wisconsin.

636.

They are not closely related to the European badger but share similar behaviors and ecological roles.

637.

American badgers have a distinctive odor, which is caused by scent glands located near their anus. This scent is used for territorial marking and communication.

638.

The badger's fur is dense and has a mix of guard hairs and underfur, providing insulation and protection from the elements.

639.

American badgers are excellent burrowers, capable of digging tunnels as deep as 10 feet (3 meters) and several yards long.

640.

They are known to exhibit playful behavior, especially among young badgers, engaging in wrestling and chasing games.

641.

American badgers have been observed using tools, such as using sticks or rocks to help dig out prey from burrows.

642.

They are relatively silent animals but can make a variety of vocalizations, including grunts, snarls, hisses, and growls.

643.

American badgers have a powerful bite and can deliver a strong jaw grip, allowing them to immobilize prey quickly.

644.

They have specialized cheek teeth adapted for crushing and grinding tough food items.

645.

Badgers have a high tolerance for venomous snake bites and have been known to attack and kill venomous snakes, such as rattlesnakes.

646.

American badgers have an excellent sense of direction and can navigate back to their burrow even when displaced or transported long distances.

647.

They have a unique hunting strategy called "sit-and-wait," where they patiently wait near the entrance of a burrow and ambush their prey as it emerges.

648.

American badgers are known to engage in "scent rolling," where they rub their bodies on strong-smelling substances, possibly as a way to mark their territory or mask their own scent.

649.

They have a relatively low metabolic rate, allowing them to conserve energy when food availability is limited.

650.

American badgers have long been depicted in Native American art and folklore, symbolizing strength, resilience, and adaptability.

651.

Francis Hopkinson was one of the signers of the United States Declaration of Independence.

652.

He was born on September 21, 1737, in Philadelphia, Pennsylvania.

653.

Hopkinson came from a highly educated family, and his father, Thomas Hopkinson, was a prominent lawyer and judge.

654.

He received a classical education and attended the College of Philadelphia, which later became the University of Pennsylvania.

655.

Hopkinson studied law and was admitted to the bar in 1761, establishing a successful legal career.

656.

In addition to being a lawyer, Hopkinson was a polymath and had a deep interest in various fields, including music, literature, and science.

657.

He was a skilled musician and composer, known for his compositions and performances on the harpsichord and organ.

658.

Hopkinson's musical talents led him to be appointed as the first organist at Christ Church in Philadelphia.

659.

He is credited with being the first American-born composer to create a secular songbook, "Seven Songs for the Harpsichord or Forte Piano."

660.

Hopkinson's literary pursuits included writing poetry and essays, some of which were published in prominent newspapers and literary journals.

661.

He was a member of the American Philosophical Society and corresponded with notable figures like Benjamin Franklin and Thomas Jefferson.

662.

Hopkinson's involvement in politics grew during the American Revolution. He became an outspoken critic of British policies and an advocate for American independence.

663.

In 1776, Hopkinson was appointed to the Continental Navy Board, where he played a crucial role in designing the United States flag.

664.

He is often attributed as the designer of the first official American flag, although historical records regarding his exact contributions are debated.

665.

Hopkinson proposed the use of stars in the flag to represent each state, as well as alternating red and white stripes.

666.

Hopkinson played a significant role in the legal and political aspects of the Revolutionary War. He served as a judge, a delegate to the Continental Congress, and a member of the Pennsylvania state legislature.

667.

He was a strong proponent of the abolition of slavery and worked to advance anti-slavery legislation in Pennsylvania.

668.

Hopkinson's legal career flourished, and he became a respected judge in Pennsylvania, serving on the Pennsylvania Supreme Court from 1779 to 1789.

669.

In 1789, President George Washington appointed Hopkinson as a federal judge for the District of Pennsylvania, making him one of the first federal judges in the United States.

670.

He remained in this position until his death in 1791 at the age of 53.

671.

Hopkinson's legal opinions were known for their clarity and adherence to constitutional principles.

672.

He was also an advocate for intellectual property rights and played a crucial role in establishing copyright law in the United States.

673.

Hopkinson was a talented satirist and wrote several political satires during his lifetime, including "The Battle of the Kegs," which poked fun at British attempts to destroy American ships during the Revolutionary War.

674.

He was a strong supporter of a strong central government and actively promoted the ratification of the United States Constitution.

675.

Hopkinson was a devout Christian and was involved in various religious and charitable organizations in Philadelphia.

676.

He was one of the founding members of the American Academy of Arts and Sciences.

677.

Hopkinson was known for his wit and humor and was often called the "wit of the Revolution."

678.

He had a reputation as a skilled orator and was often called upon to deliver speeches at public events.

679.

Hopkinson's contributions to American independence were recognized by his peers, and he was appointed as a delegate to the Continental Congress in 1776.

680.

Hopkinson was the only person to have signed the Declaration of Independence, the Articles of Confederation, and the United States Constitution.

681.

He was an advocate for strong diplomatic relations and served as the United States' first Secretary of Foreign Affairs under the Articles of Confederation.

682.

Hopkinson was known for his sharp intellect and quick wit, making him a formidable debater and contributor to political discourse.

683.

He was a proponent of the separation of powers and believed in the importance of checks and balances in government.

684.

Hopkinson had a close friendship with Thomas Jefferson and corresponded with him regularly on matters of politics and philosophy.

685.

He was known for his elegant and refined writing style, which made his speeches and essays highly influential.

686.

Hopkinson's financial situation suffered in later years, and he faced financial difficulties due to a failed land speculation venture.

687.

Despite his financial struggles, Hopkinson maintained his commitment to public service and continued to contribute to the development of the young nation.

688.

He had a deep love for the arts and sciences and actively supported cultural institutions in Philadelphia.

689.

Hopkinson's legacy as a polymath and contributor to various fields of knowledge has earned him a place among the intellectual elites of his time.

690.

He had a reputation for fairness and impartiality as a judge, and his decisions were often well-reasoned and grounded in legal principles.

691.

Hopkinson's legal and political career was marked by a commitment to justice and equality, and he advocated for the rights of all citizens.

692.

He was known for his patriotism and dedication to the principles of liberty and self-governance.

693.

Hopkinson's contributions to the American flag's design and symbolism have had a lasting impact on American culture and national identity.

694.

He was a strong supporter of education and believed in the importance of an educated citizenry for the success of the new republic.

695.

Hopkinson's writings and speeches are still studied today for their insights into the political and intellectual climate of the Revolutionary era.

696.

He was a strong advocate for religious freedom and the separation of church and state, believing that individual conscience should guide matters of faith.

697.

Hopkinson's impact on American history extends beyond his role as a signer of the Declaration of Independence. His contributions to law, music, and literature continue to be celebrated.

698.

His descendants have continued to be influential in various fields, including politics, law, and academia.

699.

Hopkinson's life and achievements have been commemorated in various ways, including the naming of buildings, schools, and scholarships in his honor.

700.

He is remembered as a dedicated patriot, a brilliant mind, and a key figure in the founding of the United States of America.

701.

Jedediah Huntington was born on August 4, 1743, in Norwich, Connecticut.

702.

He came from a prominent and influential family in Connecticut, with his father serving as a judge and his brother as a member of the Continental Congress.

703.

Huntington graduated from Harvard College in 1761 and pursued a career as a merchant before the American Revolution.

704.

He played a significant role in the Revolutionary War, serving as a colonel in the Continental Army.

705.

Huntington was known for his bravery and leadership on the battlefield, particularly during the Battle of Long Island in 1776.

706.

He commanded a regiment of Connecticut troops and played a crucial role in defending New York City against the British.

707.

In recognition of his military service, Huntington was promoted to the rank of brigadier general in 1777.

708.

He participated in several key battles of the Revolutionary War, including the Battles of Saratoga and Monmouth.

709.

Huntington was a trusted and loyal officer, earning the respect and admiration of his fellow soldiers and commanders.

710.

He was known for his strategic thinking and tactical skill, often making critical decisions in the heat of battle.

711.

Huntington's leadership extended beyond the battlefield. He served as a member of the Connecticut General Assembly and later as a judge.

712.

In 1780, he was appointed as a delegate to the Continental Congress, where he actively participated in debates and discussions on matters of national importance.

713.

Huntington played a significant role in shaping the structure and governance of the newly formed United States.

714.

After the war, he returned to his hometown of Norwich, where he became involved in various civic and philanthropic activities.

715.

Huntington served as the collector of customs for the port of New London, Connecticut, from 1789 until his death.

716.

He was a founding member of the Connecticut Society of the Cincinnati, an organization for Revolutionary War veterans.

717.

Huntington was a strong advocate for education and helped establish the Norwich Free Academy, which still exists today as a prestigious public high school.

718.

He was also a supporter of religious freedom and played a key role in the separation of church and state in Connecticut.

719.

Huntington was a close friend and confidant of General George Washington, with whom he corresponded frequently during and after the war.

720.

He maintained an active interest in military affairs and was involved in planning and organizing the state militia.

721.

Huntington's military career and contributions to the American Revolution were widely recognized and celebrated during his lifetime.

722.

He was honored with various awards and accolades for his service, including a sword presented to him by the Marquis de Lafayette.

723.

Huntington was known for his integrity and moral character, earning him the trust and respect of his peers and fellow citizens.

724.

He was deeply committed to the ideals of liberty and democracy, and his actions reflected his dedication to the cause of American independence.

725.

Huntington was a devoted family man, married to Anne Fanning Huntington, with whom he had several children.

726.

He was an avid reader and had a wide range of interests, including history, politics, and philosophy.

727.

Huntington's writings and correspondence provide valuable insights into the political and social climate of the Revolutionary era.

728.

He was a strong advocate for the rights of soldiers and veterans, working to ensure their proper compensation and care.

729.

Huntington's legacy extends beyond his military and political achievements. He was also known for his generosity and philanthropy, supporting various charitable causes.

730.

His contributions to the early years of the United States helped shape the nation and establish its principles of liberty and self-governance.

731.

Huntington's name is commemorated in various ways, including the naming of streets, parks, and historical markers in his honor.

732.

He is buried in the Old Norwichtown Cemetery in Norwich, Connecticut, where his grave is marked by a monument.

733.

Huntington's life and career have been the subject of historical research and analysis, shedding light on the challenges and triumphs of the Revolutionary era.

734.

His leadership and dedication to the cause of American independence continue to inspire generations of Americans.

735.

Huntington's portrait can be found in various museums and historical institutions, serving as a visual representation of his role in shaping the nation.

736.

He is often remembered as a courageous and honorable military leader, whose contributions to the Revolutionary War were instrumental in securing American independence.

737.

Huntington's correspondence with other prominent figures of the time, including George Washington and John Adams, provides valuable insights into the workings of the early American government.

738.

He was known for his unwavering commitment to the principles of freedom and justice, fighting for the rights of all citizens.

739.

Huntington's military strategies and tactics were praised for their effectiveness and efficiency, contributing to the success of the Continental Army.

740.

He was respected by his troops for his fairness, compassion, and dedication to their well-being.

741.

Huntington played a crucial role in maintaining morale and discipline within the army, earning the trust and loyalty of his soldiers.

742.

He was actively involved in the planning and execution of military campaigns, providing valuable insights and recommendations to his superiors.

743.

Huntington's leadership skills extended beyond the battlefield. He was a skilled negotiator and diplomat, representing American interests in various diplomatic missions.

744.

He was a strong advocate for the establishment of a strong central government and played a key role in the ratification of the United States Constitution.

745.

Huntington's commitment to public service continued after the Revolutionary War. He served as a judge, contributing to the development of a fair and just legal system.

746.

He was known for his ability to bring people together and find common ground, making him an effective mediator and peacemaker.

747.

Huntington's contributions to the early American government and legal system have had a lasting impact on the nation's development.

748.

He was a firm believer in the power of education and actively supported the establishment of schools and educational institutions.

749.

Huntington's dedication to public service and his country's well-being earned him the respect and admiration of his contemporaries.

750.

His life and achievements serve as a reminder of the courage, sacrifice, and perseverance of the Founding Fathers in their quest for freedom and independence.

751.

Onion Portage Archeological District is located along the Kobuk River in the Northwest Arctic Borough of Alaska.

752.

The site is named after the wild onions that grow abundantly in the area during the summer months.

753.

The district encompasses a vast area of approximately 70 acres and includes a series of archaeological sites.

754.

It has been inhabited for over 12,000 years, making it one of the oldest continuously occupied sites in the Arctic.

755.

Onion Portage is a significant archaeological site for studying the prehistoric cultures of the region, particularly the ancient hunting and gathering traditions.

756.

Excavations at the site have uncovered a wealth of artifacts, including stone tools, hunting implements, pottery, and ceremonial objects.

757.

The archaeological remains found at Onion Portage provide valuable insights into the lifeways and social organization of early human populations in the Arctic.

758.

The site is particularly known for its well-preserved archaeological stratigraphy, allowing researchers to reconstruct the site's history in detail.

759.

Onion Portage is associated with the Paleo-Arctic Tradition, characterized by the use of stone tools and the hunting of large mammals.

760.

It is believed that the site was used as a seasonal hunting camp, where ancient people would gather during the migration of caribou herds.

761.

The site's location along the Kobuk River made it an ideal spot for hunting and fishing, providing a reliable food source for the inhabitants.

762.

The area surrounding Onion Portage is rich in wildlife, including caribou, moose, bears, and various bird species.

763.

The site's importance was recognized in 1978 when it was listed on the National Register of Historic Places.

764.

The district is managed by the National Park Service as part of the Kobuk Valley National Park.

765.

Onion Portage has served as a cultural and spiritual site for indigenous peoples for thousands of years, and it continues to hold significance for local Native communities.

766.

The site is also important for understanding the effects of climate change on the Arctic ecosystem and its inhabitants.

767.

Archaeological research at Onion Portage has revealed evidence of long-distance trade networks, suggesting connections with other distant cultures.

768.

The site's significance extends beyond its archaeological value. It holds cultural, historical, and spiritual importance for the local Iñupiat people.

769.

Onion Portage is a place of storytelling and cultural traditions, where knowledge and oral histories are passed down through generations.

770.

The district's archaeological sites are marked by depressions, fire hearths, and remnants of ancient structures.

771.

The preservation of the site's archaeological remains is a priority, and ongoing research and conservation efforts are conducted to protect its integrity.

772.

The Onion Portage Archeological District offers a unique opportunity for visitors to learn about the ancient cultures that once thrived in the Arctic.

773.

Guided tours and interpretive programs are available, providing insights into the site's history and significance.

774.

The district's remote location and pristine wilderness offer visitors a chance to experience the natural beauty of the Arctic landscape.

775.

The surrounding Kobuk Valley is home to diverse wildlife, including migratory birds, musk oxen, and wolves.

776.

Onion Portage serves as a reminder of the enduring connection between indigenous peoples and their ancestral lands.

777.

The site's archaeological discoveries have contributed to our understanding of human migration patterns and the peopling of the Americas.

778.

The district has attracted researchers from various disciplines, including archaeologists, anthropologists, and ecologists.

779.

Onion Portage is an important site for studying the interaction between humans and their environment in the Arctic over thousands of years.

780.

The site's cultural and historical significance has been recognized by the Iñupiat people, who actively participate in its preservation and interpretation.

781.

Onion Portage is a testament to the resilience and adaptability of human communities in harsh Arctic environments.

782.

The site's archaeological findings have shed light on the technological advancements and cultural innovations of ancient Arctic peoples.

783.

Onion Portage is a place of cultural continuity, where traditions and customs have been passed down through generations.

784.

The district's archaeological sites are fragile, and visitors are encouraged to respect and preserve the integrity of the site.

785.

The site's proximity to the Kobuk River provides opportunities for boating, fishing, and other recreational activities.

786.

The district's landscapes and natural features have inspired artists, photographers, and writers, capturing the essence of the Arctic wilderness.

787.

Onion Portage is a place of archaeological mystery, with ongoing research efforts seeking to unravel its secrets and uncover new insights.

788.

The site's archaeological discoveries have challenged previous assumptions and expanded our knowledge of Arctic prehistory.

789.

Onion Portage is a place of reverence and reflection, where visitors can connect with the rich cultural heritage of the region.

790.

The district's archaeological sites offer a glimpse into the lives of the people who once called the Arctic home.

791.

The significance of Onion Portage extends beyond its borders, contributing to the broader understanding of human history and cultural diversity.

792.

The district's archaeological remains are fragile and vulnerable to erosion and climate change, necessitating ongoing conservation efforts.

793.

The site's archaeological significance has been recognized internationally, attracting researchers and scholars from around the world.

794.

Onion Portage is a testament to the enduring relationship between humans and the natural world, highlighting the interdependence of ecosystems and cultures.

795.

The district provides opportunities for hands-on learning and engagement with archaeology, offering educational programs for students and visitors.

796.

Onion Portage serves as a gathering place for cultural events, celebrations, and ceremonies that celebrate the traditions and heritage of the Iñupiat people.

797.

The site's archaeological discoveries have challenged prevailing theories about the peopling of the Americas and the adaptation of human communities to extreme environments.

798.

The district's archaeological sites offer a glimpse into the complex social structures and cultural practices of ancient Arctic societies.

799.

Onion Portage is a place of discovery and exploration, with ongoing archaeological research uncovering new insights into the region's past.

800.

The site serves as a reminder of the importance of preserving and protecting our cultural heritage for future generations.

801.

The American Kestrel (Falco sparverius) is a small and colorful bird of prey found throughout North and South America.

802.

It is the smallest falcon species in North America, measuring about 9-12 inches in length.

803.

The male American Kestrel has striking plumage, with a rusty-red back, slate-blue wings, and a white and black face pattern.

804.

Female American Kestrels have a brown back and wings, with dark streaks on their underparts.

805.

American Kestrels are highly adaptable and can be found in a variety of habitats, including open grasslands, farmlands, forests, and urban areas.

806.

They are known for their remarkable hunting skills, primarily feeding on small mammals, birds, insects, and reptiles.

807.

American Kestrels are aerial hunters and are capable of hovering in mid-air while searching for prey.

808.

They have excellent eyesight, enabling them to spot small prey from a distance of up to 100 feet.

809.

American Kestrels are cavity nesters and often use old woodpecker holes, natural tree hollows, or nest boxes for breeding.

810.

The female lays a clutch of 3-7 eggs, which are incubated by both parents for about 28-31 days.

811.

The chicks are altricial, meaning they are born naked and helpless, relying on their parents for food and protection.

812.

American Kestrels are known for their distinctive vocalizations, including high-pitched calls and rapid chattering sounds.

813.

They are highly territorial birds and will defend their nesting sites
and hunting territories from intruders.

814.

American Kestrels are migratory birds, with some populations
traveling long distances during the winter months.

815.

Their migratory patterns vary across their range, with some
individuals staying resident throughout the year.

816.

American Kestrels are known for their "kiting" behavior, where they
hover in the air while facing into the wind, using it to their advantage
during hunting.

817.

They have a fast and agile flight, capable of reaching speeds of up to
40 miles per hour.

818.

American Kestrels have a lifespan of about 5-10 years in the wild,
although some individuals have been known to live longer.

819.

They face threats from habitat loss, pesticide use, and competition
for nesting sites from other cavity-nesting species.

820.

American Kestrels are important indicators of ecosystem health, as
they rely on healthy prey populations and suitable habitats.

821.

They play a significant role in controlling rodent populations, acting as natural pest control agents for farmers and agricultural areas.

822.

American Kestrels are known to exhibit sexual dimorphism, with males being smaller and more colorful than females.

823.

They are capable of adapting their hunting strategies to different prey availability and environmental conditions.

824.

American Kestrels are diurnal birds, active during the daytime and resting or roosting at night.

825.

They have sharp and curved beaks, well-suited for tearing apart their prey.

826.

American Kestrels have a unique ability to see ultraviolet light, which helps them detect urine trails left by small mammals.

827.

They have a characteristic hunting behavior called "tail-wagging," where they rapidly flick their tail up and down while perched, possibly to attract insects or small prey.

828.

American Kestrels communicate with each other using a variety of visual displays, including wing-flapping, head-bobbing, and aerial acrobatics.

829.

They have an average wingspan of about 20-24 inches, allowing for swift and agile flight.

830.

American Kestrels have a keen sense of hearing, enabling them to locate prey even in tall grass or dense vegetation.

831.

They are known to cache excess food, storing it for later consumption.

832.

American Kestrels have a complex courtship display, with the male performing aerial acrobatics and offering food to the female.

833.

They are known to engage in cooperative hunting, where multiple individuals work together to catch larger prey.

834.

American Kestrels are protected under the Migratory Bird Treaty Act in the United States.

835.

They have been the subject of scientific research and conservation efforts to understand their population dynamics and address threats to their survival.

836.

American Kestrels have been successfully bred in captivity for educational and conservation purposes.

837.

They are popular among birdwatchers and photographers for their striking appearance and interesting behaviors.

838.

American Kestrels are often used as ambassadors for bird education programs, showcasing the beauty and importance of raptors in ecosystems.

839.

They have been featured in traditional Native American folklore and are regarded as symbols of power and agility.

840.

American Kestrels have been known to exhibit site fidelity, returning to the same nesting sites year after year.

841.

They have been observed using man-made structures, such as powerline poles and billboard signs, as nesting sites.

842.

American Kestrels have a unique flight pattern, with rapid wingbeats interspersed with short glides.

843.

They are known to perform "stoop" flights, where they dive steeply towards the ground to catch prey.

844.

American Kestrels are highly adaptable to human-altered landscapes and can be found in suburban and urban areas.

845.

They are sometimes referred to as "Sparrow Hawks" due to their small size and hunting behavior targeting small birds.

846.

American Kestrels have been used in falconry, a traditional practice of training birds of prey for hunting.

847.

They are susceptible to pesticide accumulation, as they may consume prey that has been exposed to toxic chemicals.

848.

American Kestrels have been studied for their migration patterns, with individuals tracked using satellite telemetry.

849.

They are known to exhibit courtship feeding, where the male presents food to the female as part of the mating ritual.

850.

American Kestrels are fascinating and iconic birds, embodying the beauty, grace, and adaptability of the raptor family.

851.

The American Oystercatcher (Haematopus palliatus) is a large shorebird species found along the coasts of North and South America.

852.

They have distinctive black and white plumage, with a long reddish-orange beak and bright yellow eyes.

853.

American Oystercatchers are highly specialized feeders, primarily consuming bivalve mollusks such as oysters and clams.

854.

They use their strong beaks to pry open the shells of their prey, hence the name "oystercatcher."

855.

American Oystercatchers are monogamous birds, forming long-term pair bonds that can last for multiple breeding seasons.

856.

They are known for their loud, distinctive calls, which are often described as a loud, piercing "wheep-wheep" sound.

857.

American Oystercatchers are territorial birds and fiercely defend their nesting sites from intruders, including other birds and predators.

858.

They build their nests on the ground, typically in sandy or gravelly areas near the coast.

859.

The female lays a clutch of two to four eggs, which are incubated by both parents for about 25-30 days.

860.

Both parents actively participate in raising the chicks, including feeding them and protecting them from potential threats.

861.

American Oystercatchers are considered a symbol of coastal ecosystems and are often used as indicators of the health of coastal habitats.

862.

They are migratory birds, with some populations traveling long distances between their breeding and wintering grounds.

863.

American Oystercatchers have a wingspan of about 3-4 feet, allowing for efficient flight and foraging along the shoreline.

864.

They are excellent swimmers and can navigate through coastal waters to find suitable foraging areas.

865.

American Oystercatchers have a lifespan of about 10-20 years in the wild, depending on various factors such as predation and habitat availability.

866.

They are known to form loose flocks outside the breeding season, gathering in larger groups to feed and roost.

867.

American Oystercatchers have a high-pitched alarm call that alerts nearby birds to potential danger.

868.

They have a unique way of foraging called "hammering," where they strike their beaks repeatedly on the ground to locate hidden prey.

869.

American Oystercatchers have been observed using tools, such as rocks or shells, to aid in opening stubborn bivalve shells.

870.

They are protected under various conservation acts and international agreements due to declining populations and habitat loss.

871.

American Oystercatchers play an important ecological role by controlling the populations of bivalve mollusks, helping maintain a balance in coastal ecosystems.

872.

They are highly sensitive to disturbance and habitat degradation, making them valuable indicators of the impacts of human activities on coastal areas.

873.

American Oystercatchers have a strong fidelity to their breeding sites, often returning to the same nesting areas year after year.

874.

They have been studied extensively to understand their behavior, migration patterns, and population dynamics.

875.

American Oystercatchers are susceptible to predation by larger birds of prey, such as eagles and hawks.

876.

They have been the focus of conservation efforts, including habitat restoration and predator control, to enhance their breeding success.

877.

American Oystercatchers are known to engage in "broken-wing" displays, where they feign injury to distract predators away from their nests or chicks.

878.

They have a well-developed visual system, allowing them to spot potential threats or prey from a distance.

879.

American Oystercatchers have been observed using specific feeding techniques, such as "probing" or "hammering," depending on the availability of prey and the type of substrate.

880.

They are social birds and often form loose breeding colonies, where multiple pairs nest in close proximity to each other.

881.

American Oystercatchers have been affected by habitat loss, including the destruction of coastal marshes and nesting areas due to human development.

882.

They are known to exhibit site fidelity, returning to the same breeding sites and wintering grounds year after year.

883.

American Oystercatchers have been successfully reintroduced to certain areas where their populations had declined.

884.

They are diurnal birds, being most active during daylight hours and resting or roosting during the night.

885.

American Oystercatchers have a streamlined body shape and long legs, allowing them to move swiftly and efficiently along the shoreline.

886.

They have excellent camouflage, with their black and white plumage blending in with the rocks and sand of their coastal habitats.

887.

American Oystercatchers have been observed engaging in courtship displays, including aerial flights, ritualized postures, and vocalizations.

888.

They are known to migrate along specific flyways, following well-established routes between their breeding and wintering grounds.

889.

American Oystercatchers have a low reproductive rate, with only a few offspring successfully reaching adulthood each year.

890.

They have been the subject of various research projects, including studies on their breeding biology, population genetics, and habitat requirements.

891.

American Oystercatchers have been featured in art, literature, and cultural traditions, symbolizing the beauty and diversity of coastal environments.

892.

They are often associated with seashore landscapes and are considered iconic birds of the coastal regions they inhabit.

893.

American Oystercatchers have been successfully bred in captivity as part of breeding programs aimed at reintroducing them into suitable habitats.

894.

They have been used as indicator species to assess the impacts of climate change and sea-level rise on coastal ecosystems.

895.

American Oystercatchers have a unique feeding adaptation called a "laterally compressed bill," which allows them to apply strong force to pry open the shells of bivalve prey.

896.

They are known to engage in "mobbing" behavior, where they collectively harass and drive away potential predators, such as gulls or crows.

897.

American Oystercatchers have been documented using innovative foraging techniques, such as dropping shells from a height to break them open.

898.

They are capable of flying long distances without rest, enabling them to undertake extensive migrations between their breeding and wintering grounds.

899.

American Oystercatchers have been studied using satellite telemetry to track their movements and better understand their migration patterns.

900.

They are captivating and charismatic birds, capturing the imagination of birdwatchers and nature enthusiasts with their striking appearance, unique behaviors, and vital role in coastal ecosystems.

901.

Samuel Huntington was an American statesman and jurist who played a significant role in the early years of the United States.

902.

He was born on July 16, 1731, in Windham, Connecticut.

903.

Huntington was a descendant of one of the original settlers of Connecticut, and his family had a long history of public service.

904.

He studied law and was admitted to the bar in 1754, practicing law in Connecticut.

905.

Huntington served as a delegate to the Continental Congress from 1775 to 1784, playing an active role in the American Revolution.

906.

He signed the Declaration of Independence in 1776, representing Connecticut.

907.

Huntington served as the president of the Continental Congress from 1779 to 1781, during a critical period in the Revolutionary War.

908.

As president of the Continental Congress, he presided over the adoption of the Articles of Confederation, the first constitution of the United States.

909.

Huntington played a key role in ensuring the stability and continuity of the Continental Congress during a time of great challenges and uncertainty.

910.

After the Revolutionary War, Huntington served as the first Chief Justice of the Connecticut Supreme Court, a position he held from 1784 until his death.

911.

He was known for his fair and impartial decisions as a judge, earning the respect of his peers and colleagues.

912.

Huntington was a proponent of a strong central government and advocated for the ratification of the United States Constitution.

913.

He played a crucial role in securing Connecticut's ratification of the Constitution, which helped pave the way for its eventual adoption.

914.

Huntington was a trusted advisor and confidant to many of the Founding Fathers, including George Washington and John Adams.

915.

He was highly regarded for his intelligence, wisdom, and sound judgment, making him a respected figure in the early years of the nation.

916.

Huntington was known for his humility and modesty, often downplaying his own achievements and giving credit to others.

917.

Despite his many responsibilities and commitments, Huntington remained dedicated to his family and was a loving husband and father.

918.

He had a deep sense of civic duty and believed in the importance of public service for the betterment of society.

919.

Huntington was a staunch supporter of religious freedom and played a role in ensuring that the principle was enshrined in the First Amendment of the United States Constitution.

920.

He believed in the principles of democracy and the rule of law, striving to uphold the ideals of the American Revolution throughout his career.

921.

Huntington was an advocate for the abolition of slavery and spoke out against the institution, even though it was prevalent in some parts of the country at the time.

922.

He believed in the power of education and promoted the establishment of schools and colleges to provide opportunities for learning and intellectual development.

923.

Huntington was well-versed in classical literature and history, and his knowledge and intellectual pursuits informed his approach to governance and law.

924.

He was a proponent of strong states' rights within the framework of a unified nation, striking a delicate balance between local autonomy and federal authority.

925.

Huntington's leadership during the American Revolution and his commitment to the cause of independence earned him the respect and admiration of his contemporaries.

926.

He was known for his calm demeanor and steady resolve, even in the face of adversity and challenging circumstances.

927.

Huntington played a critical role in the early establishment of the federal government, contributing to the shaping of the nation's institutions and policies.

928.

He was a dedicated public servant and believed that government should serve the best interests of the people and promote the common good.

929.

Huntington's legal expertise and keen understanding of constitutional law made him a valuable asset in the early years of the United States.

930.

He was involved in drafting and revising important legislation, contributing to the development of a strong and stable legal system.

931.

Huntington's contributions to the nation were recognized and appreciated, and he was often called upon to provide guidance and advice on matters of governance and policy.

932.

He played a role in the negotiation of treaties and diplomatic efforts, helping to establish diplomatic relations and secure the young nation's place in the international community.

933.

Huntington's dedication to public service extended beyond his official roles, and he actively participated in community affairs and charitable endeavors.

934.

He believed in the importance of civic engagement and encouraged fellow citizens to actively participate in the democratic process.

935.

Huntington's legacy as a Founding Father and a champion of liberty and justice continues to be celebrated and remembered today.

936.

He left a lasting impact on the legal and political landscape of the United States, contributing to the foundations of the nation's democratic system.

937.

Huntington's commitment to the principles of freedom and equality inspired future generations of leaders and activists.

938.

His contributions to the Continental Congress and the drafting of the Constitution laid the groundwork for the democratic institutions that still govern the United States today.

939.

Huntington's life and achievements serve as a reminder of the sacrifices made by the early patriots and the enduring values they fought for.

940.

He believed in the power of reason and dialogue and advocated for peaceful resolutions to conflicts, both domestically and internationally.

941.

Huntington's writings and speeches offer valuable insights into the thinking and perspectives of the Founding Fathers, shedding light on the motivations behind their actions.

942.

He believed in the importance of checks and balances in government, advocating for a system that prevents the concentration of power in the hands of a few.

943.

Huntington was a strong advocate for the separation of powers and believed that each branch of government should have defined roles and responsibilities.

944.

He was known for his eloquence and persuasive speaking abilities, using his words to rally support for causes he believed in.

945.

Huntington's commitment to public service and the common good was unwavering, even in times of personal hardship and sacrifice.

946.

He was a man of integrity and honesty, guided by a strong moral compass in his decision-making.

947.

Huntington's contributions to the nation's founding and governance were recognized by his contemporaries and continue to be celebrated by historians and scholars.

948.

He believed in the importance of a strong national defense and supported efforts to establish and maintain a capable military.

949.

Huntington's dedication to the principles of liberty and self-governance inspired others to fight for their rights and freedoms.

950.

His life and legacy serve as a testament to the enduring values of the American Revolution and the ongoing quest for a more perfect union.

951.

The Palugvik Site is an archaeological site located on St. Lawrence Island in Alaska.

952.

It is known for its rich cultural and historical significance, providing valuable insights into the ancient indigenous cultures that inhabited the region.

953.

The site was first discovered in the 1950s and has since been the subject of numerous archaeological excavations and studies.

954.

Palugvik is believed to have been occupied by the ancient Thule people, who were skilled hunters and gatherers.

955.

The site contains multiple dwelling structures, indicating a complex social organization and settlement pattern.

956.

Excavations at Palugvik have uncovered a wide range of artifacts, including tools, pottery fragments, and bone remains.

957.

The artifacts suggest a subsistence economy based on hunting marine mammals, fishing, and gathering wild plants.

958.

Palugvik is situated in a unique environmental setting, with access to both the Bering Sea and the Chukchi Sea, providing abundant resources for the ancient inhabitants.

959.

The site's strategic location would have allowed the Thule people to exploit the rich marine resources and engage in trade and cultural interactions with neighboring communities.

960.

The artifacts found at Palugvik indicate a high level of craftsmanship and technological expertise, with stone tools and bone implements demonstrating the ingenuity and skill of the ancient inhabitants.

961.

The site also contains evidence of ritual practices, including burial grounds and ceremonial structures.

962.

Excavations have revealed the presence of animal bones, indicating the importance of hunting in the subsistence activities of the Thule people.

963.

The discovery of harpoon heads, fish hooks, and fishing implements suggests that fishing played a significant role in their daily lives.

964.

Palugvik has provided valuable information about the Thule people's adaptations to the harsh Arctic environment, including their use of materials such as walrus ivory and whalebone for tools and shelter construction.

965.

The site's archaeological findings have contributed to our understanding of the ancient trade networks and cultural connections that existed in the region.

966.

Palugvik serves as an important site for studying the cultural and technological transitions that occurred in the Arctic during the prehistoric period.

967.

The site has helped archaeologists reconstruct the dietary habits and food preferences of the ancient inhabitants, shedding light on their subsistence strategies.

968.

Palugvik's location on St. Lawrence Island has made it a focal point for studying the migration patterns and interactions of ancient peoples in the Bering Strait region.

969.

The preservation of organic materials at Palugvik, such as bone and wood, has allowed researchers to conduct detailed analyses and radiocarbon dating to establish the chronology of human occupation.

970.

The site's archaeological findings have challenged some previously held theories about the timing and nature of human migration to the Americas.

971.

Palugvik's significance extends beyond its archaeological value, as it is also recognized for its cultural importance to the Yupik and Inupiaq people who continue to inhabit the region.

972.

The site is a testament to the rich cultural heritage and ancestral connections of the indigenous communities in Alaska.

973.

Palugvik has been a site of collaboration between archaeologists and local communities, fostering mutual understanding and respect for the cultural significance of the area.

974.

The study of Palugvik has contributed to the broader field of Arctic archaeology and the understanding of human adaptations to extreme environments.

975.

The site's archaeological remains provide a tangible link to the past and help preserve the memory of the ancient inhabitants who once thrived in the area.

976.

Excavations at Palugvik have revealed evidence of house structures, including stone foundations and remnants of organic materials, offering insights into ancient architecture and construction techniques.

977.

The site's proximity to the coast and marine resources suggests that the Thule people had a deep knowledge of the surrounding ecosystem and its seasonal variations.

978.

Palugvik has been a site of ongoing research and fieldwork, with new discoveries and interpretations continually adding to our understanding of the ancient cultures that inhabited the area.

979.

The site's location within the Bering Land Bridge National Preserve ensures its protection and preservation for future generations.

980.

Palugvik serves as a reminder of the enduring presence and resilience of the indigenous peoples in the Arctic, highlighting their deep connection to the land and their cultural heritage.

981.

The site has yielded important information about the technology and tool-making techniques of the Thule people, including the use of ground stone tools and the crafting of intricate hunting implements.

982.

Palugvik's archaeological record has provided valuable insights into the social organization and cultural practices of the Thule people, including their systems of kinship and trade networks.

983.

The discovery of pottery fragments at Palugvik suggests the development of ceramic technology among the ancient inhabitants, indicating their cultural and technological advancements.

984.

The site has also yielded artifacts associated with personal adornment, such as bone and ivory jewelry, indicating the importance of aesthetics and self-expression in Thule culture.

985.

Palugvik has served as a source of inspiration for contemporary artists and craftspeople, who draw on the rich cultural heritage of the area in their work.

986.

The site's archaeological significance has led to its inclusion on the National Register of Historic Places, ensuring its protection and recognition as a site of national importance.

987.

Palugvik's location on St. Lawrence Island has made it an important stopover point for migratory birds, contributing to the island's rich biodiversity and ecological significance.

988.

The site's archaeological findings have provided valuable data for studying climate change and its impact on human populations in the Arctic over time.

989.

Palugvik's excavation has involved multidisciplinary research, including archaeological, ecological, and geological studies, to gain a comprehensive understanding of the site and its context.

990.

The site has contributed to our understanding of the cultural interactions and exchange of ideas that occurred between the Thule people and neighboring groups, fostering a greater appreciation for the diversity of indigenous cultures in the Arctic.

991.

Palugvik has been a site of educational and interpretive programs, engaging local communities and visitors in the exploration and appreciation of the region's cultural heritage.

992.

The site's archaeological remains offer a tangible connection to the past, allowing visitors to envision the daily lives and experiences of the ancient inhabitants.

993.

The study of Palugvik has prompted further research and exploration of other archaeological sites in the Bering Strait region, expanding our knowledge of the ancient cultures that once thrived in this remote corner of the world.

994.

The artifacts found at Palugvik have been carefully cataloged and preserved, providing a valuable resource for future generations of researchers and scholars.

995.

The site has been a source of inspiration for indigenous cultural revitalization efforts, as local communities seek to preserve and celebrate their heritage.

996.

The archaeological investigations at Palugvik have contributed to the development of innovative fieldwork techniques and methodologies for studying Arctic sites, given the unique challenges posed by the harsh environment.

997.

Palugvik's archaeological record has provided important insights into the mobility and settlement patterns of the Thule people, shedding light on their seasonal movements and adaptations to changing environmental conditions.

998.

The site has served as a venue for cultural events and celebrations, where indigenous traditions and practices are shared and passed down to younger generations.

999.

Palugvik's archaeological findings have fostered a greater appreciation for the ancient craftsmanship and artistic expressions of the Thule people, whose skills and creativity are evident in the artifacts they left behind.

1000.

The ongoing research and exploration at Palugvik continue to unravel the mysteries of the ancient Thule culture, ensuring that their legacy lives on and contributes to our understanding of human history in the Arctic.

ESCRITOS DE UM DOIDINHO

A ESQUINA

1ºedição
2021

Luciano Plínio

Projeto Editorial por Dez Páginas

Diagramação:Thamiris Pinotti

Capa: Thamiris Pinotti

Revisão: Clara Giron

Ilustrações: Marlon Thor

@projetos_dezpaginas
dezpaginas@gmail.com